In This Issue

PIVOT MAGAZINE

Founder
Jason Miller

President
Juddene Villarin

Web Master
Joel Phillips

Designs
ReliableStaffSolutions.com

Copyright © 2025 PIVOT

ISBN: 978-1-957217-63-5

Contact

Jason Miller
Founder
1151 Eagle Drive #345
Loveland, CO 80537
jason@strategicadvisorboard.com

Chris O' Byrne
Editor-in-Chief
chris@jetlaunch.net
520-261-3101

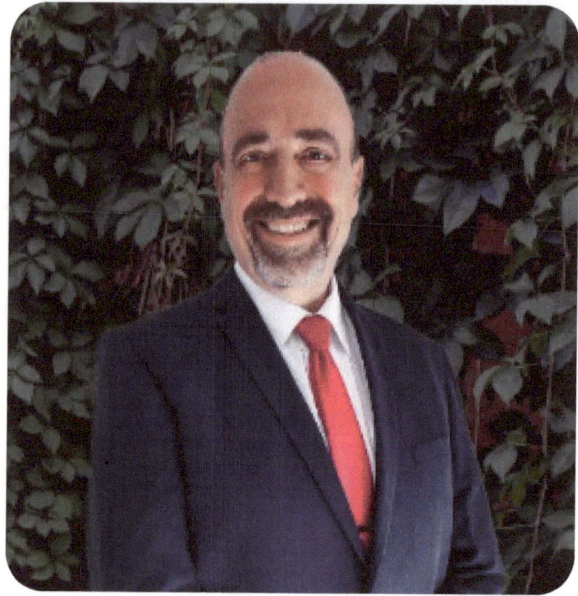

From the Editor

There's something powerful about starting with intention. It's about carving space to refocus before the pace picks up again.

This issue of PIVOT was built in that spirit. You'll find the kind of thinking that doesn't shout but shifts. Leaders who are moving forward by trimming back. Entrepreneurs who are asking smarter questions, not chasing louder answers.

Real momentum rarely begins with chaos. It begins with clarity.

We curated voices that reflect that. People building with discipline, scaling with purpose, and staying sharp in seasons that demand more than performance. They're not here to impress. They're here to make progress that lasts.

Wherever you are in your leadership cycle—starting fresh, resetting focus, or adjusting course—I hope these pages meet you with the right kind of tension. The kind that stretches you forward.

Here's to what's next, and to building with intention at every step.

Chris O'Byrne
Editor-in-Chief

From the Desk
Of The President

Leading with Intention in a Season of Reset

There's something about this season—a natural shift that invites reflection and intentional growth. For leaders, it's not just about spring cleaning—it's about strategic clarity.

At *PIVOT*, that's exactly what this issue is about. We're doubling down on thoughtful momentum, clear decisions, and leadership that doesn't wait for permission. You'll find insights from entrepreneurs and executives who are simplifying to scale, letting go to grow, and proving that progress often starts quietly.

To our contributors—your bold thinking continues to shape this platform. And to our readers—you are the reason PIVOT moves forward. Your hunger to grow, refine, and lead better defines every page.

As you step into a new quarter, ask yourself:
- What clarity do I need before chasing growth?
- What noise can I clear to create room for sharper thinking?

Clarity isn't a luxury—it's the first move.
Let this be your season of reset. Refocus your energy, raise your standards, and recommit to building something that scales with purpose.

JUDDENE VILLARIN *J.V.*

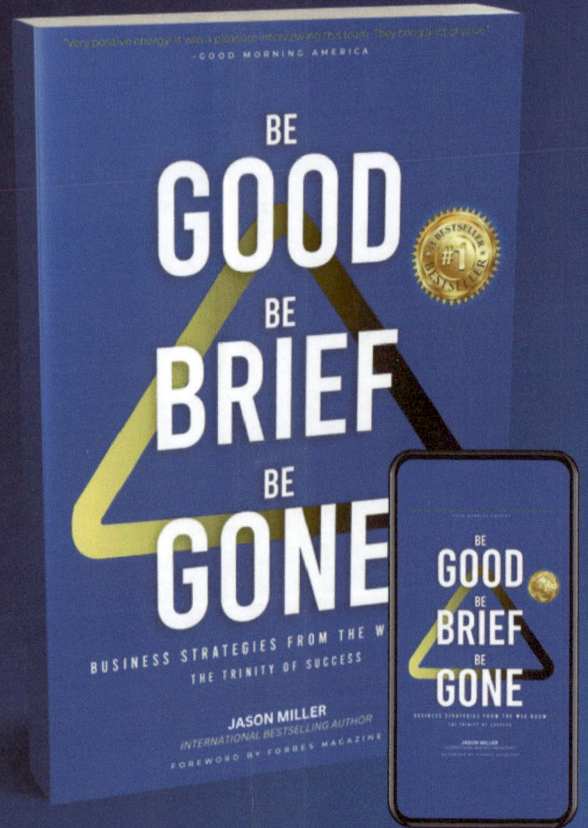

Power, Pressure, and The $40 Million Question

Inside the Trump Administration's Legal Crackdown and What It Means for Corporate America

In March 2025, the Trump administration issued one of its most controversial executive orders yet—a directive targeting law firms engaged in litigation against the federal government. Framed as an effort to curb "frivolous lawsuits" and protect taxpayer dollars, the order instructed Attorney General Pam Bondi to identify firms allegedly abusing the legal process. The stakes were clear: firms named in the order risked losing federal contracts, facing public scrutiny, and having their access to government agencies restricted.

At the center of the controversy stood Paul, Weiss, Rifkind, Wharton & Garrison LLP, a global legal powerhouse known for its influence in corporate law, civil rights advocacy, and political litigation. The firm's name was reportedly included in internal DOJ discussions—setting the stage for a high-stakes confrontation between legal independence and political leverage.

Rather than fight, Paul Weiss opted for a deal. According to multiple sources, the firm agreed to provide an estimated $40 million in pro bono legal services for administration-backed initiatives and conduct an internal audit of its employment policies. Most notably, the firm committed to halting its diversity, equity, and inclusion (DEI) initiatives—a decision that stunned the legal community and sparked nationwide debate.

Behind closed doors in a sleek Manhattan boardroom, firm partners debated late into the night. One partner reportedly tapped the DEI program folder and said, "If we don't give them this, we give them everything else." That moment, by many accounts, marked the tipping point.

A Legal Giant, A Political Flashpoint

Founded in 1875, Paul Weiss is no stranger to high-profile cases. It has defended Fortune 100 companies, advised world governments, and taken landmark civil rights cases to the Supreme Court. The firm played a leading role in Brown v. Board of Education, and more recently, defended Apple in a major antitrust lawsuit. Its lawyers move between the corridors of Wall Street and Capitol Hill, commanding both respect and influence. Which is why the firm's perceived capitulation to Trump's demands felt seismic.

"This isn't about politics. This is about precedent," said one former partner, who spoke under the condition of anonymity. "Paul Weiss has a legacy. That legacy now

includes folding under pressure." The firm's DEI policies had long been a point of pride—publicly promoted and tied to internal hiring benchmarks. To dismantle those programs, even under executive pressure, sent a message far beyond 1285 Avenue of the Americas.

"This isn't about politics. This is about precedent. Paul Weiss has a legacy. That legacy now includes folding under pressure." — Former Paul Weiss Partner

The Fallout: Legal Community Strikes Back

Industry Echoes and Law School Currents

The ripple effects didn't end with angry letters and public statements. Within weeks of the Paul Weiss announcement, several elite law schools reported emergency curriculum revisions—adding modules on executive overreach, constitutional balance, and ethics in federal litigation.

At NYU School of Law, Dean Clarissa Grant held a town hall to address concerns from students over future employment prospects. "We are not preparing students simply for a job," she said. "We are

preparing them for a moral profession. That distinction matters now more than ever."

The tension has also ignited debates within legal hiring pipelines. Associates and recent grads are beginning to privately question whether aligning with firms compliant to government ideology undermines their long-term values—or legal integrity. Some firms have even paused campus recruiting pending clarity on how federal relationships will evolve.

The backlash was swift. Over 100 former attorneys from Paul Weiss issued a joint letter condemning the agreement. Law school deans and civil rights groups followed with statements expressing concern over government interference in private firm governance. Legal trade publications lit up with commentary framing the event as a turning point in how law firms navigate politically hostile terrain.

"Coerced compliance" became the phrase of the week.

In an editorial for The National Law Journal, former federal judge Karen Traynor called the deal "a surrender to authoritarian impulses." She warned that once legal firms are reviewing their own federal ties and litigation strategies to assess risk.

Playing Hardball: Trump's Strategic Leverage

The executive order is just the latest in a series of aggressive moves by the Trump administration to reshape the business and legal landscape. With mounting lawsuits against federal agencies and a Republican-controlled Congress backing his use of executive authority, the former president has leaned into a combative strategy: reward loyalty, punish dissent.

From a business lens, the play is bold. By leveraging federal contracting power, the administration is signaling to every company, firm, and consultant doing business with Washington: know which side you're on.

For critics, this crosses a dangerous line. "This is more than a legal dispute—it's the federal government weaponizing access," says Lila Emerson, a political ethics professor at Georgetown University. "It's not just about what firms do. It's about what they're allowed to believe and promote."

Supporters of the administration, however, argue that the executive order is long overdue. "Taxpayers shouldn't be funding firms that work

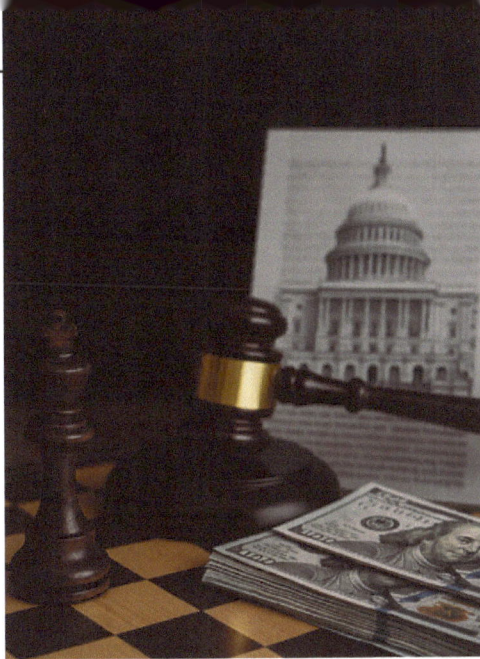

against the government's interest," said an anonymous White House official. "This is about accountability, not ideology."

Corporate Risk, Reputation, and the DEI Divide

The decision to abandon DEI initiatives has raised questions far beyond the legal field. Corporate leaders, especially in industries with visible social impact policies, are watching closely. If one of the most influential firms in the U.S. can be pressured to reverse course on DEI, what's to stop the same tactics from reaching Fortune 500 boardrooms?

The debate is polarizing. Some executives see it as an overdue correction to what they view as performative compliance. Others warn of reputational damage and eroded employee trust.

"DEI isn't just about optics anymore. It's a trust signal to

both talent and stakeholders," says Adrienne Miles, a corporate communications strategist who advises multinational brands. "If firms like Paul Weiss are forced to walk that back, they risk more than a headline—they risk culture collapse."

A recent Deloitte survey found that 68% of employees consider a company's stance on equity and inclusion when deciding whether to stay with an employer. The Paul Weiss controversy may prove to be a bellwether moment in how firms navigate the intersection of politics, policy, and people.

Business Lessons: When Compliance Meets Compromise

For general counsel and risk officers, the real question isn't whether Paul Weiss made the right decision—it's whether they would do the same. In an era where federal contracts are gold and political pressure is growing, business leaders are being forced to reconsider how much independence they can afford.

The decision also casts a spotlight on pro bono work as political currency. Is $40 million in free legal labor a fair trade for continued access? Or is it a Trojan horse that sets a

precedent for transactional governance?

According to a senior partner at another major law firm: "It opens the door for policy blackmail. What's next—carbon audits for energy firms? ESG reviews for investors? It's a slippery slope."

What to Watch in 2025–2026: The Forecast Box

Signals and shifts general counsel are tracking next

- Client Intake Filters: Firms are quietly reconsidering which federal clients to accept—and which cases to avoid.
- Reframing DEI: Internal policies are being rebranded under terms like "cultural excellence" or "strategic alignment."
- **Legal Definitions at Stake:** Lobbyists and trade groups are pushing to narrow the meaning of "frivolous litigation" before enforcement expands.
- **New Reputation Metrics:** Stakeholders are weighing silence or compliance just as heavily as legal outcomes.

What to Watch in 2025–2026: The Forecast Box

Signals and shifts general counsel are tracking next

- Client Intake Filters: Firms are quietly reconsidering which federal clients to accept—and which cases to avoid.
- Reframing DEI: Internal policies are being rebranded under terms like "cultural excellence" or "strategic alignment."
- Legal Definitions at Stake: Lobbyists and trade groups are pushing to narrow the meaning of "frivolous litigation" before enforcement expands.
- • New Reputation Metrics: Stakeholders are weighing silence or compliance just as heavily as legal outcomes.

Media Reactions and Global Comparisons

The international media response has been just as fiery.

European legal journals like The Law Gazette (UK) and Juriste Internationale (France) have run front-page stories under headlines such as "The End of Legal Autonomy?" and "When Governments Write the Rules for Lawyers."

Legal scholars abroad have noted alarming parallels to past moments in history when state pressure shaped legal frameworks—notably in Hungary, Poland, and even 1970s Argentina. "These moments rarely begin with a bang," said Dr. Max Adler of the University of Vienna. "They begin with redefinitions. With compliance. And with silence."

While the U.S. legal structure is still robust, critics warn that moments like Paul Weiss could normalize state interference—not just for law firms, but for banks, insurers, and media companies next in line.

Precedents and Parallels: A Look Back to Move Forward

The Trump administration's tactic of targeting law firms may feel novel, but the roots of executive influence over legal and regulatory landscapes stretch deep into American political history. In 1971, for example, President Nixon sought to suppress legal dissent by attempting to manipulate the DOJ's relationship with private firms. During the Reagan years, ideological alignment was often quietly required for access to certain public-private initiatives, though the mechanisms were far subtler than Trump's overt mandates.

Fast-forward to the post-9/11 years, and legal firms found themselves navigating the Patriot Act's shifting definition of acceptable surveillance counsel. That moment shifted expectations around corporate legal compliance, embedding the idea that national interest could supersede long-standing legal norms. What differentiates the Paul Weiss moment, however, is its performative quality—it was public, transactional, and symbolically linked to the cultural fault line of DEI.

Legal historians caution that erosion of institutional autonomy rarely happens overnight. It begins, they say, with a chilling effect—one firm pulling back, one value rebranded as risk. In this case, $40 million didn't just buy services. It bought silence.

A Barometer for Corporate America

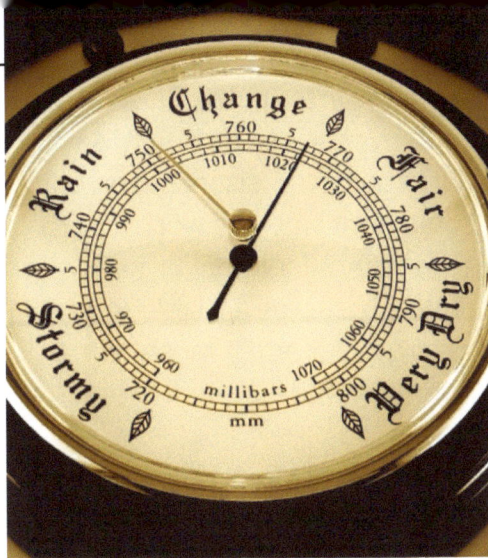

This moment with Paul Weiss may soon be studied in business schools and boardrooms not for its legal technicalities—but for its strategic implications. The firm's decision functioned as a barometer for where the winds are blowing across sectors.

As regulatory scrutiny, shareholder activism, and partisan realignment collide, corporations are asking themselves: What will we yield under pressure—and what will we protect at all costs?

Internal audits of DEI programs are being conducted with a new question in mind: Not just are we effective—but are we politically safe? Communications teams are rewriting messaging that once touted bold values into language that signals neutrality. And general counsel offices are crafting contingency plans for a future where federal contracts come with unwritten ideological clauses.

In this environment, "noncompliance" isn't about illegality—it's about identity. About whether a brand, firm, or leader signals alignment with prevailing political winds or stands quietly in opposition.

Scenarios: If This Becomes the Norm

Let's look forward. If Paul Weiss is not an exception—but the prototype—what happens next?

1. **Tiered Access to Public Contracts:** Government contracts might evolve into tiered systems—where only firms meeting certain ideological benchmarks receive the full suite of access and privilege.
2. **DEI as Liability in RFPs:** Vendors and contractors could begin masking or minimizing their equity commitments in federal RFPs (requests for proposals) to avoid disqualification.
3. **Expansion to Other Industries:** Today it's law. Tomorrow, it could be health, media, or tech. Regulatory bodies may scrutinize ESG language, political donations, or employee initiatives under the guise of neutrality.
4. **Rise of Legal and Ethical Arbitrage:** Some firms may relocate offices or re-charter operations in more ideologically aligned

jurisdictions—choosing strategic silence to survive.

Reputational Recovery: Can a Firm Rebuild After Folding?

As Paul Weiss navigates the aftermath of its public capitulation, the question looming over its future is not just legal—it's reputational. Can a firm that yielded so visibly to political pressure regain the trust of clients, recruits, and the broader legal community?

History suggests recovery is possible, but the road is long and politically fraught. Take the case of Skadden, Arps, Slate, Meagher & Flom LLP, which faced major criticism after a 2018 DOJ settlement tied to its work in Ukraine. The firm paid millions and faced public backlash—but eventually reemerged, restructured its compliance programs, and shifted its branding toward transparency and international law excellence.

For Paul Weiss, the path may look similar: a renewed investment in internal ethics protocols, increased visibility in traditionally underserved communities, or high-profile pro bono wins that lean back into the firm's social justice roots.

Reputational strategists say transparency will be key. "The worst thing any institution can do in the aftermath of a values controversy is to go quiet," says Raina Solis, a crisis management consultant who has worked with several multinational firms. "There has to be a visible return to principle—and it must be felt internally and externally."

Some suggest Paul Weiss may even reposition itself as a cautionary tale turned reform leader. That requires time, humility, and visible acts of contrition—like funding DEI education initiatives externally or publishing internal decision-making audits.

Narrative Rebuilding Through Results

Ultimately, trust is regained through action. Paul Weiss has resources, relationships, and a century-old foundation that could allow it to rebuild faster than others. But that trust will be contingent on whether the firm defines itself by its capitulation—or by what it chooses to stand for next.

The Bigger Picture: What Comes After

What began as an executive order now feels like a political litmus test. The Paul Weiss saga may ultimately become the playbook—or the cautionary tale—for how firms, and businesses at large, manage public-private pressure under an unpredictable administration.

In boardrooms across the country, the question isn't whether to engage with Washington—it's how to do so without compromising brand, values, or integrit

And if the next crisis demands more than policy compliance—if it requires silence, alignment, or public endorsement—will they resist, or recalibrate?

For Paul Weiss, the cost of staying close to power was $40 million. For others, the cost may not be measured in dollars, but in principles surrendered.

In a landscape where influence trumps precedent, the most valuable currency may no longer be legal skill or political strategy—but the willingness to choose a side.

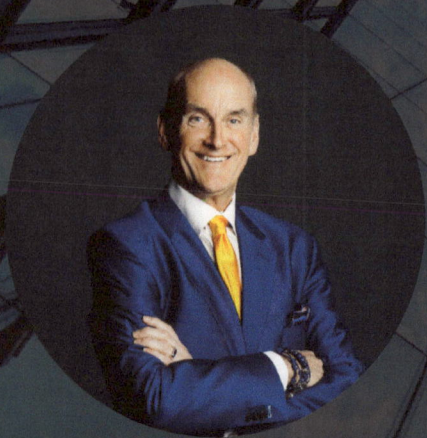

Rethinking Selling through High Trust and Value

Todd Duncan

> *"Transactions will make you a living. Relationships will make you a fortune."*

Chris O'Byrne

What was a defining moment in your early life that helped you develop into who you are now?

Todd Duncan

The first thing that comes to mind is the most unlikely gift I received on my sixteenth birthday from my grandmother. My grandmother was always a very positive person. On my sixteenth birthday, she gave me a book titled *Success Through a Positive Mental Attitude*, written by Napoleon Hill and W. Clement Stone. Most sixteen-year-olds wouldn't be reading a book on attitude, but I had experienced some heavy emotional and verbal trauma from my mother. I found myself becoming negative about that trauma and letting it define me, not knowing then what I know now.

My mother told me I would never amount to anything and that I was a failure. My grandmother saw this from a disassociated perspective, observing her daughter treating me this way. So, she gave me this book, and I devoured it. One of the quotes that became my North Star as a young person caught between adolescence and adulthood still stands out to me today. The quote was: "There is very little difference between successful and unsuccessful people. But the little difference makes a big difference. The little difference is attitude. And the big difference is whether it's positive or not."

I latched onto that quote and realized, in a rather fortunate way, that I had the power to choose my approach to the day. I could choose negativity, or I could choose positivity. I could choose to be an optimist or be defined by my mother's label of being a pessimist.

At sixteen, I started asking a question most sixteen-year-olds don't ask. In any situation that could define me as a failure, I asked, "What's good about this?" As soon as I started asking that question, I realized that any mistake I made—which, after all, is what failure is—was simply an opportunity to learn how to do something a new way. That realization was a breakthrough for me.

So, how does someone go about developing a positive mental attitude? It's not usually as simple as just flipping a switch. There's a lot of research on the subject. One book that became influential for me after I graduated college and entered the business world was *Learned Optimism* by Dr. Martin Seligman.

The emphasis is on both words—optimism and, more importantly, learned optimism. Optimism is easy to grasp: I can see something as positive or negative. The hard part is the first word: learned.

Learning how to choose positivity begins with understanding that any situation or moment is just that: a situation or a moment. How you go through that moment often defines the next moment—or the subsequent ones. A good example of this comes from a few years ago when Phil Mickelson competed at the Masters.

On Sunday morning, Mickelson was tied for tenth in the final round. He made an impressive run, and on the eighteenth hole, he had a beautiful drive just short of the bunker and an easy chip to the green. His putt, wherever the ball landed,

became one of those crowd-pleasing moments where you could tell by the roar that the ball had gotten close to the pin. He sank the putt, birdied the hole, and tied for second place.

In the clubhouse after the round, Mickelson was asked about his mindset that Sunday morning. He explained, "In golf and in life, I can't change the shot that got me here. I can't plan the shot until I've hit it. Wherever I am, whether it's ninety yards from the green or anywhere else, this is the only shot that matters." He added, "Regardless of past mistakes or future uncertainties, you have to focus on the shot in front of you."

This analogy works perfectly for people in both business and life. We have a choice in how we believe and what we think. There is always a next shot, and I can either go into the next one holding onto the mistakes of the past, or I can decide that the only shot that matters is the one I'm about to take.

This leads me to what I call belief stacking. The idea behind belief stacking is simple: When you do something well, it sets you up for the next action with greater belief, confidence, and less worry. For me, this idea became another North Star. Over time, I began to understand that failure is a friend of success. You can't define one without the other, much like you can't define night without day or loud without soft.

The good news is that doing something wrong shows you what

doesn't work, which is just as valuable as discovering what does work. We've heard countless analogies over the years that failure and success are part of the same equation. People who achieve anything purposeful or impactful, leaving a legacy, understand that it is the failure and setbacks that get you thinking about the opportunity on the other side of them—provided you interpret them in that way.

You can look at any technological breakthrough from any time in history and see mistakes along the way. The key is that people learn from them. The wrong way to do something can actually be the right way because it teaches you a better way. Once you internalize this, you learn optimism. There are no setbacks, only speed bumps.

This is a powerful enough lesson that we could end the interview here, and people would still gain so much from it.

Chris O'Byrne

You are known for being an expert salesperson. How did you get into sales?

Todd Duncan

I think most people get into sales the way I did, as a miserable, unequipped, and scared-to-death sales professional. The real turning point came when I realized how to transform that mindset into a jet stream that has allowed me to impact people worldwide.

I was originally going to be a doctor. I had enrolled at Colorado State University, where I was studying pre-med. My father, a doctor, had influenced my decision. However, I also enjoyed skiing, so I joined the ski team. In my first pre-med semester, I skied seventy-four days, which, as you can imagine, took time away from studying. By the end of that semester, my GPA was a resounding 1.2, and my father was paying out-of-state tuition. He gently told me that he wouldn't continue paying for my tuition if I didn't bring my grades up.

I promised him I would improve, and I brought my GPA up to 1.9 the following semester. I thought, "That's a fifty-point improvement, Dad—give me a break." So, I went home for summer break, where I had a conversation with my father that would change everything. He invited me to chat while picking oranges in the driveway one afternoon. He said, "You don't have to be a doctor just because I am." This was the first time I had heard that. As the oldest son, I had always thought I should follow in his footsteps.

Then, he said something that hit me hard: "You probably won't be a good doctor." When your dad says that lovingly, it's a bit of a reality check.

I asked, "Well, what should I do?"

My father, as fathers do, offered some advice. "You're really good with people, and you're good in business. You started a landscaping company at sixteen, and when you were nine, you sold more candy than anyone at Little League. You should be in business."

That's when he told me about three prestigious business schools in California—Stanford, USC, and Cal State Fullerton. He made it clear that he wouldn't pay for either of the first two but that Fullerton, with its affordable state tuition, was the best option. So, I enrolled. Three years later, I graduated with honors—on the dean's list with a 3.9 GPA. That's when the stars began to align.

Just a month after graduation, at a Fourth of July party hosted by my Little League coach and his wife, I had a conversation that would set the course for my career. Don, my coach, asked what I planned to do next. I told him I wasn't sure, and he mentioned that he had a real estate and mortgage company. "What was your major?" he asked. I told him it was business. "And your minor?" he asked. I told him it was finance. "You should be a mortgage professional," he told me.

That was it; getting into business was that simple. I interviewed the next day and started that Monday as a commission sales rep, with a ninety-day guarantee of $1,500 monthly. After that, I'd "eat what I killed."

Looking back, I wasn't equipped for the job. I understood business and finance but didn't understand marketing, branding, or some of the fundamentals that helped me get to where I am today. The first year was tough. I made about seven hundred cold calls and was rejected by everyone. Then, one day, I went to the beach to clear my head and called a friend whose father owned a real estate company. I asked if I could watch how people secured buyers for financing by calling on real estate agents.

About thirty vendors came through from 1:00 p.m. to 4:00 p.m., all looking for business. One was a man named John Barnes, who struck me immediately. He was 6'5", dressed impeccably in a blue suit and tie, and had a calm, confident demeanor. He approached the receptionist and said, "My name is John Barnes, and I have an appointment with Paula Richardson."

I watched him for forty-five minutes, and he didn't rush. Unlike me, who had been calling on a hundred people in the same amount of time, he spent those forty-five minutes with just one person. When he left, he extended his hand and said, "I really enjoyed our time. I look forward to a mutually profitable business partnership."

That was a turning point. I followed him out to the parking lot and introduced myself. I asked him, "What did you do? I've been rejected eight hundred times in the last two weeks, but you didn't seem to face any rejection."

He said, "I had an appointment because someone told us we should meet. I was confident she would say yes, and I spent forty-five minutes figuring out how to add value to her life and business."

I asked him, "Can you mentor me?"

John gave me a test question: "What's more important— pursuing transactions or building relationships?"

At the time, I was thinking about transactions, but I wisely asked, "What's the difference?"

John responded, "Transactions will make you a living. Relationships will make you a fortune."

At twenty-three, that moment changed everything. Over the next twelve years, I financed six thousand properties and became the number one mortgage originator in the country. This success was possible because I had a mentor, and as is often the case with those who have been mentored, I felt the responsibility to mentor others.

That's how *High Trust Selling* was born.

At twenty-five, I was the number one person in my company. My manager, Bob, asked me to teach a group of new salespeople, and I spent two days doing so. The feedback was incredible: "You've changed my life," they told me. I thought, No, you changed your life; I just gave you ideas to help you change.

Later, I was invited by a title company to speak to five hundred real estate agents. I was still a mortgage professional at the time, helping people buy and finance property. Years later, my title partner invited me to a seminar hosted by Tom Hopkins. Tom spoke to thousands of salespeople, and at 9:30 a.m., he said, "The key to life is waking up every day knowing you're answering your calling."

That was when I realized that my calling wasn't doing loans but educating people. After the seminar, I told Tom I felt called to be a speaker. He asked me, "When are you going to be one?"

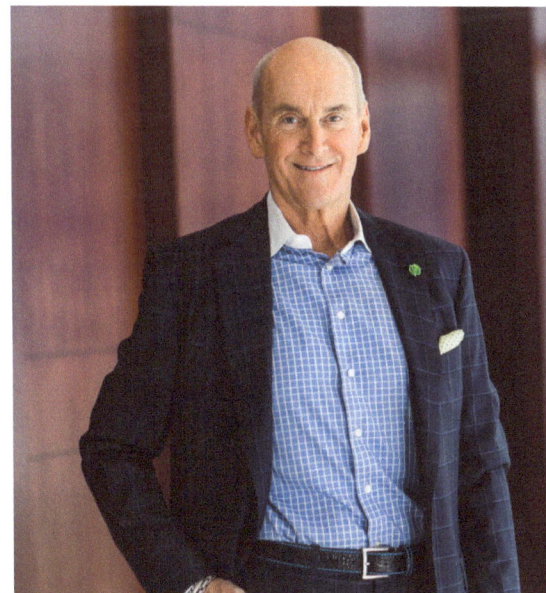

I responded, "I'm not sure."

Tom said, "Well, you should determine that right now."

At that moment, I committed to becoming a speaker and set the date—July 8. Tom told me to write the date in my planner and put it on the back of my business card. "If you don't call me by that date, I'll call you," he said. That conversation was a game-changer.

So began *High Trust Selling*. The premise is simple: If you sell when trust is low, and tension is high, you'll face resistance, objections, and stalls. However, you'll get acceptance if you focus on building trust and lowering tension. My mentor's method—building relationships—taught me that I should first understand what my clients wanted rather than pushing my agenda. When trust is high, sales naturally follow.

That's the backbone of *High Trust Selling*: fewer clients, more impact. It's about nurturing relationships and focusing on building trust instead of pushing transactions. If you do that, you won't have to sell anything; you'll simply create an emotional impact, and your clients will trust you to do business with them.

That's the reversal of the old mindset.

Twenty-two years after *High Trust Selling* was published, it continues selling every month.

I'm grateful it has become a roadmap for sales professionals worldwide.

Chris O'Byrne

There are many selling systems or methods out there. Are they all basically the same?

Todd Duncan

There are probably three types of authors: the innovator, the influencer, and the copier. I would describe myself as an innovator of high trust. I believed that I had a place in history, teaching not only an emotional way to succeed in business and life but also a formulaic approach. However, it's important that this formula doesn't become tedious or boring like an accounting formula.

Let me give you an example. The same individual, Tom Hopkins, who asked me when I would become a speaker, eventually became a friend. I had started my company, and over time, I had the opportunity to share something with him. I said, "When I first heard you speak, you told the audience, 'If it takes you ten calls to get a deal worth $1,000, and each time someone says no, you should visualize $100 going into your pocket. Stay optimistic and keep selling.'"

I told him, "I think that's a flawed approach."

Now, Tom is still alive, a good friend, and probably one of the greatest sales trainers ever.

However, when I told him my opinion, he asked, "Do you have a better idea?"

I replied, "First of all, it's very hard for people to hear 'no,' get rejected, and positively say, 'I've got $100 in my pocket.' My idea is this: Instead of trying to push through rejection, why not get good enough or even great enough so you can make one call and secure $1,000? Because if nine people say no, that first impression is blown. Think about the psychology of having to get yourself excited for a second attempt after such a blow."

The problem is that people don't thrive on rejection because they don't frame it correctly. As we discussed earlier, rejection can signify something being done incorrectly. When I ask millions of salespeople worldwide, "How many of you have ever experienced call reluctance?" every hand goes up. When I ask why, the common answer is fear. Fear of what? The fear of hearing no more often than hearing yes.

This brings me to a critical point: It's not about dwelling on rejection. Instead, we need to focus on improving our approach and conversion strategies. To reference Phil Mickelson, I can't change the rejection from yesterday or the previous hour, but I can adjust it now. I want to avoid repeating the same mistakes that led to rejection and then trying to get positive in a moment that may feel like a failure. The key to overcoming call reluctance is understanding that it's a byproduct of ineffective conversion and approach systems.

Be a Genius Entrepreneur

Live a life of freedom, optimum performance, and passion.

Genius Entrepreneur group

- ✓ Weekly zoom meetings
- ✓ Community of Support
- ✓ Marketing opportunities

Genius Entrepreneur Program

- ✓ Brand Strategy
- ✓ Signature Program
- ✓ Rogram curriculum

Genius Speaker Series

- ✓ Keynote Speaker training
- ✓ Tedx Training
- ✓ Sell from stage

SHELBY JO LONG
BUSINESS COACHING

Shelbyjolong.com | Business Dynamics

What would happen if you had called excitement instead of call reluctance? Imagine if your entire sales team was so confident and well-equipped that they sought bigger, better, and more influential prospects. When skills are low, standards drop, and salespeople target easier leads. However, by developing confidence, they could raise the bar.

Imagine I'm about to call Chris, but I'm plagued by doubt. Yesterday was rough, and I've been rejected so many times. If I approach this call with that mindset, I'm doomed. I've already given away my power to an event that hasn't even occurred yet. It's counterproductive to let past rejections define future opportunities.

Tom once called my approach naive, but I proved him wrong the following year when I went through Dale Carnegie's School of Selling. After thirteen weeks of training and preparation, I became the sales talk champion because I had the best approach to sales conversion. I always remember that tall guy, twelve years prior, who gave me the initial advice.

There are many ways to sell, but understanding principles is key. Emerson Harrington, a nineteenth-century expert on efficiency, famously said that many methods can work as long as the principles are right. However, without the right principles, no method will succeed. High Trust Selling is based on five critical principles:

1. Everything can be improved.
2. There is no success without failure.
3. Emotional connection deepens relationships and accelerates performance.
4. Move from competence to confidence, consistency, and compound results.
5. Accountability is more important than action, but nothing happens without action.

If you follow these five principles, you'll find various ways to succeed, but certain consistencies will never change. One of the most important aspects of high trust is that loyalty is a two-way street. You can't ask for loyalty from a client unless you produce enough value for them to stay loyal.

Salespeople often forget to nurture existing clients and instead chase after new prospects. However, nurturing the one hundred clients you've built relationships with is far more efficient than trying to find one hundred new ones each year. Referrals make a huge difference, increasing trust and lowering resistance to the sales process.

A key element of building trust is listening—really listening. Salespeople must be competent enough to create trust, which comes from asking insightful, game-changing questions and, most importantly, listening to the answers. When a prospect feels heard, they'll close themselves because they feel valued and believe you have a solution to their problem.

Take, for example, real estate agents. I would ask every client: "What are three problems you're facing right now that you want to solve within twelve months? Or, based on where you are today, where would you like to be in three years, and how can I help?" These questions are not about selling; they're about understanding the client's needs and building an emotional connection.

Emotional connection is crucial, particularly for high-ticket items. The higher the price, the more important the emotional connection becomes. We tell clients, "Turn down the promotion and turn up the emotion." By connecting emotionally, conversion rates rise. If a prospect sees that you genuinely understand their needs, they'll likely say yes.

A great sales question is this: "What would it mean to you, personally, in three years if the three things you're working on were fixed and working perfectly?" The answers will often reveal what is most important to the prospect, which creates an emotional anchor that drives the decision.

However, this process also requires practice. Successful salespeople know that practice makes perfect, and this concept can be likened to the "dress rehearsal" law in *High Trust Selling*: practicing your approach elevates your performance. Joe Montana, for example, practiced fifty hours a week for a one-hour football game. Salespeople, too, must practice more than they perform to succeed. If you don't practice, you'll look unprepared when it's time to make a sale.

The goal is for 91 percent of salespeople to meet or exceed their sales goals, which can happen through confidence, competence, and continuous improvement.

Chris O'Byrne

Can you tell me more about myfuel.io and what you're doing there?

Todd Duncan

One of the things that people who continuously advance in their careers have in common,

and not just because of need, is their core drive and motivator. When I started the Duncan Group in 1994, after twelve years of helping people finance real estate, my objective was simple: I wanted to give people a roadmap that would lead them to success in both business and life with a high degree of certainty.

Over time, the company evolved into a major event organizer, incorporating speeches, coaching, and more. When COVID-19 hit, we had a contract for a live event in October. The pandemic was officially declared in February 2020, though we had heard rumors earlier. I remember wondering what we would do when there was no certainty that live events would be allowed that year. Unfortunately, we couldn't exit the contract because of an "Act of God" clause, which required a thirty-day notice for release. While I considered COVID-19 an act of God, the lawyers didn't see it that way.

I told my team, "We need to pivot." We needed to immediately switch gears and, instead of holding a live event, make the decision to livestream Sales Mastery. The event typically drew 2,500 to 3,000 attendees in person each year.

So, we found a studio that had worked on Netflix productions. The studio was equipped with real-time animation, 3D imagery, and cutting-edge technology. It was one of the most advanced broadcast

studios in America. We followed the same format as we would for a live event, but instead of having people in the venue, we had our instructors come to the studio in Atlanta and broadcast the event.

At the end of the event, I asked my tech team about the numbers. Matt, my lead technician, told me that at no point during the event did fewer than 15,000 devices stay connected. The peak occurred on day two, with 44,000 devices connected. We don't know exactly how many individual viewers there were or how many group "watch parties," but we know we reached seventeen countries—a feat we could never have accomplished without COVID.

This brings me back to our earlier conversation about attitude. I can't change COVID, but I can change what I do during COVID. I can't control the market, but I can control my actions within it. When it was over, I told my wife, "I'm going to create a digital technology company. We will become the largest digital video distribution company in the world."

She asked, "What?"

I said, "Imagine if we were purposeful. If 44,000 people attended our event, just think about what we could achieve." That's when I had the idea: What if we could make learning fast, easy, affordable, and as appealing as Netflix while also making it as performance-enhancing as Peloton? That would be something huge, something worldwide.

It wasn't just about me anymore. One person approached me at the end of the event and said, "This was great, but I'm not sure where to start." That's when it hit me: I had a moral and ethical responsibility to ensure people learned and had a clear roadmap for implementation. The faster I could provide them with that roadmap, the better off they would be—and the better off I would be.

Then, I thought about Netflix's success. Behind every show on Netflix, there are thousands of people working to create something great. What if I could bring together one hundred of the world's best instructors, speakers, and authors? My partner Alex and I took this idea further. We realized that based on the "more from less"

philosophy, I knew one person who could help us open the doors to these instructors—my publisher.

Our initial goal was to have twenty-five instructors by the end of last year, but we ended up with seventy-one. This illustrates an important point: How fast you can accomplish your goals often depends on who you know.

Next, we decided to reinvent the way people learn. Traditional long-form content is often too expensive and not flexible enough. One size doesn't fit all. People are at different points in their lives and careers and need to learn differently. So, we applied AI technology to make personalized recommendations— like what Netflix or Amazon does when they suggest other content based on what you've watched or purchased.

We created three hundred lessons, and our goal is to have one thousand. Each lesson is designed to be between three and six minutes long, reflecting

the eighty-twenty principle— focusing on what's essential. We aim to make learning fun, fast, and easy. We've also made it so affordable that anyone around the world can access it.

Yesterday, we onboarded 2,500 new users in just one day. Our platform offers one hundred languages through AI translation, which makes it accessible to an even wider audience. There are no boundaries anymore. The

platform is called Fuel (you can check it out at myfuel.io), and it's available on-demand, accessible from any device, anywhere, at any time.

When you think about sales organizations, where 91 percent of their sales teams failed to meet their goals last year, how much would it be worth to invest in each person's development?

One manager told me a story about a sales employee who asked for a book allowance. This was the first time he had encountered such a request. The employee said, "I want to be one of the best sales performers in the company.

Will you give me $20 a month to buy a book?"

That moment made me realize how much we lose when salespeople aren't excited, confident, and prepared. Our instructors have written 309 books, and we've condensed these into micro-content. For just $22 a month, anyone can access over three hundred of these impactful books, which have already influenced nearly half a billion people worldwide. At the end of the day, it's about how we take content, strip it down, and make it easy to understand and implement. Fuel is based on the belief that if you're not healthy off the job, you won't be happy on the job. Personal development is the key to happiness; happiness is a by product of personal growth.

My father, a doctor, took me to his medical school when I was thirteen and showed me the cadaver room. He told me, "Do you know why doctors work on dead bodies? Because when we go live, we don't want to make mistakes." Looking back on that, I realize that sales people must practice before going live.

They need to role-play, handle tough situations, and prepare because their clients deserve the best. If salespeople aren't equipped, they're effectively failing the same way a doctor would if they weren't trained.

Action Steps

1. Shift your focus to relationship-building: The author emphasizes that building strong relationships, rather than chasing transactions, is the foundation for long-term business success. Focus on creating value and trust with your clients to foster loyalty and repeat business.

2. Adopt a positive mindset and learned optimism: The author highlights the importance of viewing challenges as opportunities and maintaining a positive attitude. Practice reframing setbacks as learning experiences to stay motivated and resilient in your business journey.

3. Refine your approach with mentorship and preparatioLearn from mentors and role models, as the author did, to develop effective strategies. Regularly practice and prepare for client interactions to increase your confidence and achieve better outcomes.

About the Author

Todd Duncan is a globally recognized High Trust Sales authority dedicated to transforming how mortgage professionals achieve higher income and more freedom. As the leading speaker and sales trainer for top-performing mortgage professionals, Todd equips the industry's elite with strategies to shift from transactional selling to building lasting, trust-driven relationships that consistently convert.

With seventeen books, including the New York Times Best Sellers Time Traps and High Trust Selling, Todd has revolutionized the sales landscape for nearly three decades. His iconic Sales Mastery Event, the longest-running and most exclusive conference in the mortgage industry since 1992, continues to be a career-defining experience. Featured on Fox, CNN, The New York Times, The Wall Street Journal, and more, Todd's innovative approach is the bridge between sales goals and personal success.

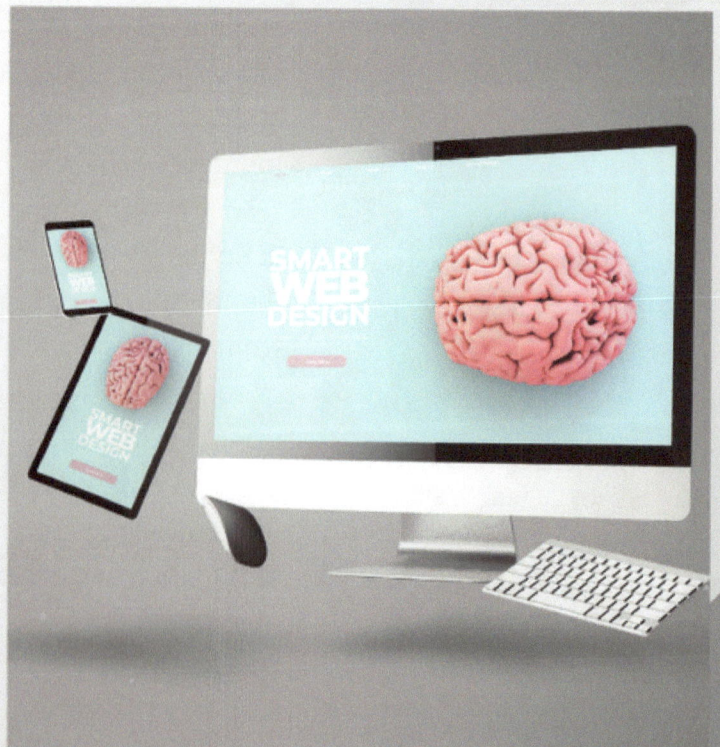

Key Legal Considerations for Growing Companies

As businesses scale and expand into new markets, understanding the complex web of legal regulations that govern their operations is critical. Whether a company is launching new products, entering new geographic regions, or even refining its internal processes, it's crucial to address key legal considerations that can make or break their success. With the heightened pressure from legal crackdowns in corporate America, navigating these issues effectively is more important than ever.

Navigating the Legal Landscape

For growing companies, the path to success isn't just about hitting revenue targets or scaling operations—it's about doing so within the confines of the law. This article explores the various legal factors businesses must keep in mind when expanding, especially under the heightened legal scrutiny that corporate America faces today. From intellectual property protection to ensuring compliance with labor laws, the growing list of legal requirements can be overwhelming. However, navigating these regulations is not optional; it is an essential step in building a business that can weather legal challenges and avoid costly penalties. This becomes increasingly important in light of regulatory changes and political pressures that affect corporate practices at every level.

1. Intellectual Property Protection

As businesses innovate, they create intellectual property (IP) in the form of patents, trademarks, and copyrights. Intellectual property protection is crucial, especially for startups and scale-ups that rely on unique ideas, products, or services to maintain their competitive edge. Without proper IP protection, companies risk having their innovations copied, resulting in potential revenue loss or brand dilution.

Case Study: In 2014, a tech

startup in the wearable fitness space was sued by a larger competitor for infringing on its patents related to sensor technology. The startup, while ultimately victorious, spent over $3 million defending itself in court. This case highlights the high stakes involved in IP protection for growing companies.

Emerging Trends: With advancements in blockchain, companies now have a more secure way to protect intellectual property. Blockchain can serve as an immutable ledger to document the ownership and transfer of IP rights, reducing the risk of theft or unauthorized use.

Practical Tip: Secure your intellectual property early. File for trademarks, copyrights, and patents as soon as you have a marketable product or service. Working with a specialized IP attorney can ensure you're adequately protected and avoid future legal headaches.

2. Compliance with Employment Laws

As your business expands, so does your workforce. This presents both an opportunity and a challenge. With growth comes an increased need for awareness of labor and employment laws, including wage and hour laws, anti-discrimination policies, and worker safety regulations. In the current climate, businesses are under more pressure than ever to ensure that their hiring practices, pay structures, and workplace policies are in compliance with federal, state, and local regulations. Failure to comply with these laws can result in costly fines, lawsuits, and damage to a company's reputation—issues no growing business can afford.

Case Study: A large retail chain was hit with a class action lawsuit after failing to classify certain employees correctly under federal wage and hour laws. The company ended up settling for $50 million, a costly reminder that compliance isn't optional.

Practical Tip: Conduct regular audits of your HR policies, and stay updated on both federal and state labor laws. Establish clear procedures for reporting complaints and ensuring that your workplace policies are in line with current legislation.

3. Contracts and Agreements

One of the most important legal considerations for any growing company is the contracts it enters into. Whether it's with employees, customers, suppliers, or partners, contracts serve as the foundation of your business relationships. Well-drafted contracts help clarify expectations, minimize risks, and protect your interests in case of disputes.

As you scale, the number of contracts will inevitably increase, and so will the complexity. Understanding the finer points of contract law—ranging from service agreements to non-disclosure agreements (NDAs)—is essential for protecting your company. Ensuring that all agreements are clear, comprehensive, and legally enforceable is crucial to avoiding misunderstandings or litigation down the road.

Case Study: A tech startup once faced a legal battle with a former partner over the terms of a joint venture agreement. The contract's vague wording led to a multi-million-dollar lawsuit that the company ultimately lost. The case demonstrated the importance of clear, precise contracts, particularly when partners and business ventures are involved.

Practical Tip: Always have a lawyer review your contracts to ensure they are airtight. Even the smallest ambiguity can lead to significant legal issues as your business grows.

4. Regulatory Compliance

Navigating government regulations is often one of the most challenging aspects of business expansion. As your company grows, you'll need to be aware of various industry-specific regulations, including environmental standards, advertising rules, consumer protection laws, and tax requirements. Non-compliance with these laws can result in fines, lawsuits, or even the suspension of business operations.

Moreover, many industries are experiencing heightened regulatory scrutiny, especially in areas like data privacy and security. Businesses are under increasing pressure to comply with strict data protection regulations, such as the General Data Protection Regulation (GDPR) in Europe or the California Consumer Privacy Act (CCPA). Failing to adhere to these laws can result in severe legal and financial penalties.

Case Study: A social media platform faced a $5 billion fine by the Federal Trade Commission (FTC) for violations related to consumer privacy under the GDPR. This fine was a stark reminder of the financial consequences of failing to comply with data privacy laws.

Emerging Trend: As data privacy becomes a focal point, businesses are being required to implement more stringent security measures to safeguard consumer information. Increasingly, businesses must think about compliance from a global perspective.

Practical Tip: Regularly review and update your privacy policies, particularly if you're handling personal customer data. Invest in cybersecurity and compliance audits to ensure that your business is adhering to all relevant regulations.

5. Dispute Resolution and Litigation

As businesses grow, the risk of disputes increases. Whether it's a disagreement with a partner, supplier, employee, or customer, conflicts are inevitable in any business. How a company handles disputes is crucial, particularly in an era where legal battles are becoming more costly and public.
Having a clear and enforceable dispute resolution mechanism in

place, such as mediation or arbitration clauses in contracts, can help resolve conflicts without the need for protracted and expensive litigation. Companies should also be prepared for the possibility of lawsuits, ensuring that they have proper legal counsel and insurance to protect against potential risks.

Practical Tip: Include dispute resolution clauses in all key contracts. Mediation or arbitration is often quicker and more cost-effective than going to court. Establish a legal contingency plan to ensure you're prepared if a dispute escalates.

6. Environmental and Sustainability Laws

For businesses operating in industries like manufacturing, retail, or energy, environmental laws play an important role. Compliance with environmental regulations, such as waste disposal laws, emissions standards, and sustainability practices, is essential for avoiding legal penalties and maintaining a positive public image.

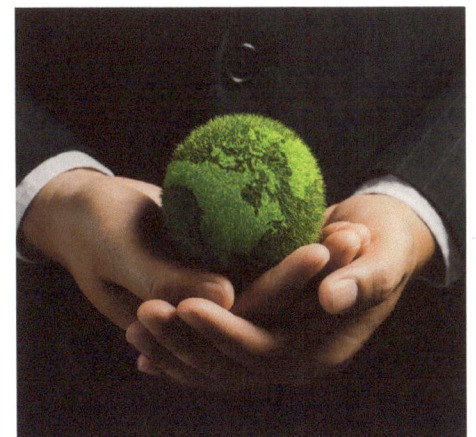

Moreover, as consumers and investors increasingly demand corporate accountability, businesses that are proactive in adopting sustainable practices may gain a competitive advantage. Understanding environmental regulations and incorporating sustainability into your business strategy can be a powerful way to not only comply with the law but also strengthen your brand's reputation.

Emerging Trend: Consumers are holding brands to higher standards in terms of sustainability. Businesses that fail to prioritize environmental accountability risk not only legal consequences but also losing market share.

Practical Tip: Stay ahead of emerging environmental regulations by joining industry groups or attending webinars on sustainability practices. Implement sustainable sourcing and manufacturing practices to mitigate environmental impact.

Legal Risks in a Changing Landscape

In recent years, corporate America has faced growing pressure from the legal system, especially with stricter regulations and increased legal crackdowns. The Trump Administration, for example, introduced various policies and executive orders that had far-reaching implications for business operations. Understanding how these legal changes impact your industry and adapting accordingly is crucial for businesses aiming to thrive in today's environment.

Legal Risks in a Changing Landscape

In recent years, corporate America has faced growing pressure from the legal system, especially with stricter regulations and increased legal crackdowns. The Trump Administration, for example, introduced various policies and executive orders that had far-reaching implications for

business operations. Understanding how these legal changes impact your industry and adapting accordingly is crucial for businesses aiming to thrive in today's environment.

Conclusion

In conclusion, growing a business successfully requires more than just effective marketing, innovation, and leadership—it also demands an in-depth understanding of the legal frameworks that govern your operations. Navigating these legal challenges, from intellectual property to regulatory compliance, is crucial for ensuring that your business remains on the right side of the law and is positioned for long-term success.

As legal pressures increase, businesses must be proactive in addressing legal considerations from the outset of their growth journey. By prioritizing legal compliance and establishing solid internal structures, businesses can protect themselves from costly mistakes and ensure they remain competitive and sustainable in an increasingly complex business environment.

DOING GOOD IS GOOD BUSINESS

SHARING THE CREDIT

Your business can give to charity without writing a check. Visit **www.SharingTheCredit.com** and start giving today.

The Balancing Act: Profit, Ethics, and Social Responsibility in Business

In today's business environment, the pressure to generate profits is intense. With increasing competition, economic uncertainty, and rapidly changing market dynamics, the focus on financial success has never been more urgent. However, in an era of heightened awareness around social, environmental, and ethical concerns, businesses are finding themselves at a crossroads: how do they balance the pursuit of profit with the demand for ethical practices and social responsibility?

This article explores the delicate balancing act that businesses must navigate, where profit, ethics, and social responsibility intersect. We will discuss the importance of aligning business goals with ethical standards, the role of corporate social responsibility (CSR), and the legal and reputational risks of failing to prioritize these considerations. By examining real-world examples and offering practical insights, we'll shed light on how companies can successfully balance these often competing demands to ensure long-term success.

The Growing Demand for Corporate Responsibility

Consumers today are more informed and engaged than ever before. They expect businesses to not only provide high-quality products and services but also to act responsibly and ethically. Social media, coupled with the rise of transparency, has shifted the power dynamics between consumers and businesses. Now, consumers can easily access information about a company's practices, from labor conditions in the supply chain to environmental sustainability efforts. This increased awareness has led to a growing demand for businesses to integrate ethical considerations into their operations.

Case Study: In 2018, Nike faced a public backlash after a controversial ad campaign featuring Colin Kaepernick. While many applauded Nike's stand on social issues, others criticized the company for engaging in what they perceived as political activism. Despite the backlash, Nike's decision to support Kaepernick's stance on social justice resonated with younger, socially conscious consumers. The company's stock price rose, and it gained increased brand loyalty from key demographics, proving that standing firm on social issues can pay off if done authentically.

This case underscores the importance of aligning business practices with social responsibility. Companies that ignore these concerns risk damaging their reputation and alienating consumers. Ethical considerations have thus become a critical component of business strategy, directly affecting the bottom line.

Profit vs. Ethics: The Age-Old Dilemma

The tension between profit and ethics is not new. Historically, businesses have been driven by the desire to maximize shareholder value, often at the expense of social and ethical considerations. However, this mindset is increasingly being questioned. The old notion that companies must choose between doing good and doing well is being replaced by the understanding that ethical

business practices can be a driver of success.

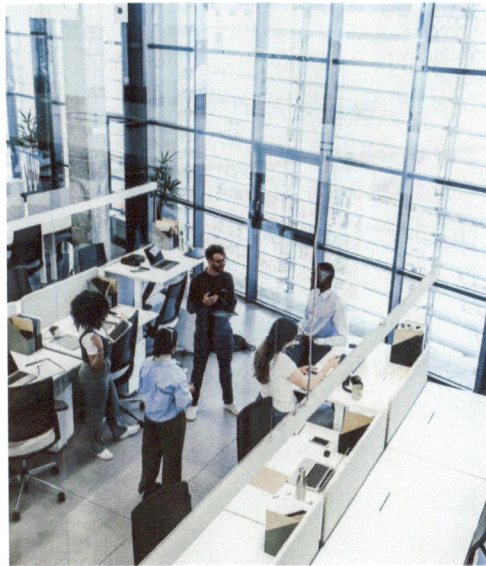

The Role of Corporate Governance in Ethical Decision-Making

Corporate governance plays a key role in this shift. Strong governance structures ensure that ethical considerations are embedded into decision-making processes, from the executive level to the operational level. Governance frameworks focused on transparency, accountability, and long-term sustainability help businesses avoid short-term profit-maximizing behavior that may harm their reputation or the community.

Increased scrutiny from regulators, shareholders, and consumers means that businesses can no longer afford to overlook the ethical implications of their actions. A failure to implement effective governance can result in costly legal battles, reputational damage, and a loss of consumer trust.

Example: In 2008, the financial industry was rocked by the global recession, largely caused by unethical practices such as subprime mortgage lending and the manipulation of financial products. The fallout from these practices led to massive bailouts, regulatory reforms, and a public outcry over corporate greed. The crisis highlighted the dangers of short-term thinking and the importance of ethical decision-making at the highest levels of business.

Corporate Social Responsibility (CSR): A Tool for Aligning Profit and Ethics

One of the primary ways businesses can balance profit and ethics is through Corporate Social Responsibility (CSR) initiatives. CSR refers to a company's efforts to take responsibility for its impact on society, the environment, and its stakeholders. These initiatives often go beyond legal obligations, focusing on voluntary actions that benefit society and the planet.

CSR programs can take many forms: from environmental sustainability efforts to charitable donations, employee volunteer programs, and fair labor practices. By integrating CSR into their business model, companies not only contribute positively to society but also enhance their brand value and customer loyalty.

The Triple Bottom Line: A concept often associated with CSR is the "triple bottom line" (TBL) framework, which advocates for businesses to focus not only on financial profits but also on social and environmental outcomes. The three pillars of TBL—profit, people, and planet—encourage companies to measure their success based on more than just financial performance.

Case Study: Unilever, a global consumer goods company, has long been a pioneer in CSR. The company's Sustainable Living Plan focuses on improving health and well-being, reducing environmental impact, and enhancing livelihoods across its supply chain. By prioritizing sustainability, Unilever has built a loyal customer base and improved its operational efficiency, demonstrating that profitability and social responsibility can go hand in hand.

The Legal and Reputational Risks of Ignoring Ethics

While the ethical benefits of CSR are clear, there are also significant legal and reputational risks for businesses that fail to prioritize ethics and social responsibility. From labor violations and environmental damage to misleading marketing practices, businesses can face legal action, hefty fines, and long-lasting damage to their reputation.

Legal Risks: In many industries, companies are required by law to comply with certain ethical standards, such as environmental regulations or fair labor practices. Failure to comply with these regulations can lead to lawsuits, fines, and regulatory action that can cost a business millions of dollars. Beyond legal requirements, businesses also face the risk of shareholder actions, particularly when unethical behavior undermines the long-term value of the company.

Reputational Risks: In today's digital world, a company's reputation is closely tied to its social responsibility efforts. A single misstep, such as failing to disclose a product's environmental impact or engaging in exploitative labor practices, can result in public backlash and a loss of consumer trust. Rebuilding a tarnished reputation can take years and may result in lost market share and revenue.

Example: In 2015, Volkswagen faced one of the largest corporate scandals in history when it was revealed that the company had installed "defeat devices" in its diesel vehicles to cheat emissions tests. The scandal cost Volkswagen billions of dollars in fines, settlements, and lost sales. The reputational damage was immense, and it took years for the company to regain consumer trust.

Ethical Leadership: The Role of Executives in Driving CSR

Ethical leadership is the cornerstone of a company's

ability to balance profit with ethics. Executives play a crucial role in setting the tone for the entire organization. When leaders prioritize ethical decision-making and integrate CSR into the business strategy, they send a powerful message to employees, stakeholders, and consumers that doing the right thing is a priority.

The Importance of Transparent Communication: Ethical leaders also understand the importance of transparency in communication.

Whether it's reporting on environmental impact, discussing labor practices, or addressing consumer concerns, transparent communication helps build trust and shows that the company is accountable for its actions.

Example: Patagonia, an outdoor apparel company, is known for its commitment to environmental sustainability and social responsibility. CEO Rose Marcario has been vocal about the company's commitment to protecting the planet, even at the cost of short-term profits.

For example, Patagonia pledged to donate 100% of its Black Friday sales to environmental causes, a decision that resonated deeply with consumers and reinforced the company's commitment to its values.

Balancing Profit, Ethics, and Social Responsibility: The Path Forward

In conclusion, businesses today are operating in an increasingly complex environment where profit, ethics, and social responsibility must coexist. To succeed in this landscape, companies must understand that ethical practices are not a barrier to profitability but rather a pathway to sustainable success. By aligning business practices with social responsibility, companies can create long-term value for shareholders, employees, and society at large.

As the demand for transparency, accountability, and sustainability continues to grow, businesses that embrace these values will not only avoid legal and reputational risks but also gain the trust and loyalty of consumers. The balance between profit and ethics is challenging, but with the right leadership, governance, and commitment to social responsibility, businesses can thrive in an increasingly ethical marketplace.

Ethical Leadership: Driving Business with Integrity

In the business world, leadership is not just about making decisions that drive profits, but about setting a standard of integrity that influences the entire organization. Ethical leadership is the foundation on which great businesses are built, and it extends far beyond the corporate boardroom. The true measure of leadership lies not only in what a leader accomplishes but in how they accomplish it.

Today's business environment is increasingly complex, and companies face heightened pressure to balance profit-making with ethical practices. This creates a unique challenge for leaders—how can they make decisions that drive growth while remaining committed to ethical standards and social responsibility? The growing importance of ethical leadership cannot be understated, as business leaders are now held to higher standards, not just in terms of financial results but also in terms of their social and ethical impact.

In this article, we will explore the concept of ethical leadership, why it matters, and how leaders can foster a culture of integrity within their organizations. We will also discuss the long-term benefits of ethical leadership and the risks businesses face when ethics are sidelined. Through examples of successful ethical leaders and organizations that have embraced integrity, we'll highlight the key elements of ethical leadership that are critical for the modern business landscape.

What is Ethical Leadership?

Ethical leadership is defined as the practice of leading by example, maintaining honesty, transparency, and integrity, and making decisions that align with moral and ethical values. Ethical leaders not only focus on achieving business goals but also consider the broader impact their decisions have on employees, customers, society, and the environment.

At its core, ethical leadership is about making decisions that are not just profitable but also responsible. These leaders are committed to upholding high standards of conduct, ensuring fairness, respecting diverse perspectives, and promoting ethical behavior at all levels of their organizations. Ethical leadership encompasses a deep sense of responsibility and a commitment to doing the right thing, even when it is difficult or unpopular.

Core Values of Ethical Leadership

1. **Integrity**: Ethical leaders act with integrity, adhering to strong moral principles in both their professional and personal lives. Integrity means being truthful, keeping promises, and acting consistently with the values you espouse.
2. **Transparency**: Ethical leaders maintain openness in their actions and decision-making processes. Transparency builds trust within organizations and with external stakeholders, creating an environment where people feel safe to voice concerns and offer solutions.
3. **Accountability**: Ethical leaders take responsibility for their actions and decisions, acknowledging mistakes when they occur and learning from them. Accountability helps foster a culture of trust and respect, where employees feel that their leaders are reliable and fair.
4. **Fairness and Justice**: Leaders who practice ethical leadership are committed to fairness. They ensure that all employees are treated equitably, regardless of their background, and that decisions are made based on merit and in the best interest of the organization.
5. **Social Responsibility:** Ethical leaders understand that businesses have a responsibility to contribute positively to society. This includes supporting environmental sustainability, ensuring fair labor practices, and engaging in community outreach.

The Importance of Ethical Leadership

In today's world, businesses face a wide array of challenges that demand strong, ethical leadership. From public scrutiny and the rise of social media to increasing regulatory oversight and consumer activism, companies must navigate these complexities with transparency and responsibility. Ethical leadership has become not just a moral obligation but a strategic advantage.

1. Building Trust and Credibility
Trust is the cornerstone of any successful business. Ethical leaders build trust with employees, customers, investors, and the broader community by making decisions that are in alignment with moral values and long-term goals. Trust is essential for fostering loyalty and collaboration within organizations, as well as for establishing positive relationships with customers and stakeholders.

Case Study: One prime example of ethical leadership is Starbucks. CEO Howard Schultz has long been an advocate for corporate responsibility, focusing on issues like fair trade, environmental sustainability, and employee welfare. His commitment to ethical leadership has helped Starbucks build a strong brand identity rooted in trust and respect, allowing the company to maintain a loyal customer base even amid increasing competition.

2. Enhancing Employee:
Engagement and Loyalty
Ethical leadership leads to higher employee engagement. When employees believe their leaders operate with integrity and fairness, they are more likely to feel motivated and committed to the company's goals. In contrast, organizations with unethical leadership often experience high turnover rates, low morale, and a lack of commitment.

Case Study: Patagonia, the outdoor apparel company, is another prime example of ethical leadership Its commitment to environmental sustainability, fair wages, and transparency in its supply chain has earned the company not only a loyal customer base but also high employee satisfaction. Employees are more likely to stay with an organization that aligns with their personal values, and this deep sense of purpose enhances overall organizational success.

3. Mitigating Legal and Reputational Risks: Companies that operate without ethical leadership are more likely to find themselves embroiled in scandals or legal troubles. Whether it's financial fraud, workplace harassment, or environmental violations, unethical leadership can expose a company to significant legal and reputational risks.

In contrast, ethical leadership helps companies mitigate these risks by ensuring compliance with laws, regulations, and industry standards. Ethical leaders create a culture where employees are encouraged to report misconduct, and where the company's values are clearly communicated and upheld at every level.

Case Study: The 2008 financial crisis serves as a powerful example of the consequences of unethical leadership. Many of the banks and financial institutions involved in the crisis were driven by short-term profit motives, disregarding ethical considerations such as fairness and transparency. The fallout from the crisis led to billions of dollars in fines and a widespread loss of trust in the financial industry.

How Ethical Leaders Drive Business Success

While ethical leadership is rooted in strong moral principles, it is also closely tied to business success. Ethical leaders understand that maintaining high standards of integrity not only benefits society but also positively impacts their companies' long-term viability.

1. Attracting and Retaining Top Talent: The best talent wants to work for organizations that share their values. Ethical leadership attracts employees who are passionate about making a positive impact. These employees are more engaged, productive, and loyal to their organizations.

2. Building Strong Customer Relationships: Today's consumers are more socially conscious and informed than ever before. They want to support businesses that are committed to ethical practices. Ethical leadership helps build strong, trusting relationships with customers, leading to greater customer loyalty and advocacy.

3. Enhancing Brand Reputation: In a world where businesses are under constant scrutiny, an ethical reputation can be one of the most valuable assets a company has. Ethical leadership strengthens brand reputation, which can lead to increased sales, greater market share, and the ability to attract investors.

4. Creating Long-Term Value: Ethical leadership focuses on long-term success rather than short-term profits. By making decisions that prioritize people and the planet as well as profits, ethical leaders ensure their organizations are sustainable, both financially and socially. Companies that adopt ethical leadership are better positioned to adapt to changing market conditions and to thrive in a world that increasingly values social responsibility.

The Challenges of Ethical Leadership

While the benefits of ethical leadership are clear, it is not without its challenges. In the face of intense pressure to meet financial goals, ethical leaders must navigate competing demands and make tough decisions that can sometimes conflict with their principles.

1. The Pressure to Compromise: In industries driven by fierce competition, leaders may feel pressure to make unethical decisions in order to gain a competitive advantage. Whether it's cutting corners to reduce costs or ignoring environmental regulations to increase production, ethical leaders must resist these pressures and prioritize the long-term health of the company.

2. The Cost of Doing the Right Thing: Ethical decisions often come with a higher price tag. Whether it's investing in sustainable manufacturing practices, ensuring fair wages for employees, or complying with stricter environmental standards, ethical choices can sometimes mean higher operational costs. Ethical leaders must make the case for these investments, demonstrating that the long-term benefits far outweigh the immediate financial costs.

3. Navigating Ethical Gray Areas: Some situations

present ethical gray areas where the right decision is not always clear. For example, a company may be faced with a decision about outsourcing jobs to a country with lower labor costs, but doing so may result in job losses for domestic employees. Ethical leaders must weigh the potential benefits and harms of their decisions, considering not just profitability but the social and environmental impact as well.

The Future of Ethical Leadership

As the business landscape continues to evolve, the demand for ethical leadership will only grow. With increasing transparency, more informed consumers, and heightened regulatory scrutiny, ethical leadership is becoming a necessity, not just a luxury. In the future, businesses that prioritize ethics and social responsibility will lead the way in creating a more equitable and sustainable world.

Conclusion

Ethical leadership is at the heart of any successful organization. By leading with integrity, transparency, and fairness, ethical leaders create lasting value for their companies, employees, customers, and society at large. While the challenges are significant, the rewards are even greater. Ethical leadership fosters trust, loyalty, and long-term success, proving that businesses can do well by doing good.

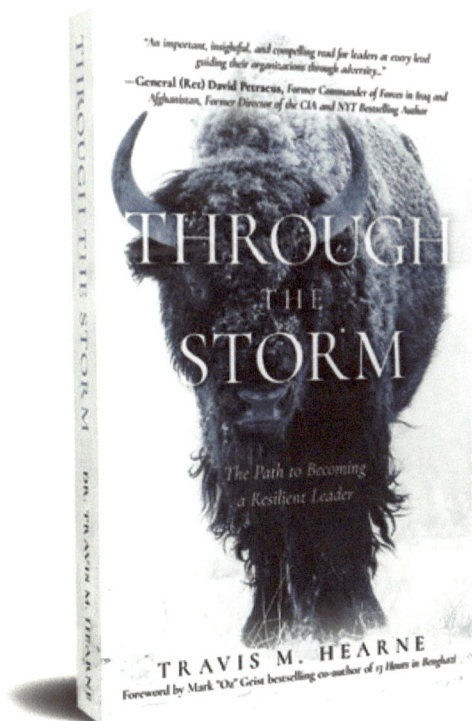

Building a Business Case for Innovation: Navigating Legal and Ethical Boundaries

Innovation is often regarded as the lifeblood of business, enabling companies to stay competitive, adapt to changing market conditions, and deliver new value to customers. But while the drive for innovation is essential, it must also be balanced with an understanding of the legal, regulatory, and ethical boundaries that govern business operations. Innovating without considering these boundaries can result in costly mistakes, lawsuits, and long-term damage to a company's reputation.

The process of building a business case for innovation is not just about generating new ideas or products. It involves aligning innovation efforts with a company's core values, ensuring compliance with relevant laws, and making decisions that benefit the company, its customers, and society at large. This article explores how businesses can successfully navigate the complexities of innovation while adhering to legal and ethical standards, and why doing so is critical for long-term success.

Understanding the Business Case for Innovation

At its core, the business case for innovation is about demonstrating how investing in new ideas, technologies, or processes will create value for the organization. Whether it's through improving efficiency, enhancing customer satisfaction, or capturing new market share, innovation has the potential to drive significant business growth. But building a compelling case for innovation requires more than just pointing to potential profits; it requires a deep understanding of the broader implications, including the legal and ethical dimensions.

Key Elements of a Business Case for Innovation

1. **Market Opportunity:** Any innovation must be rooted in a clear market opportunity. Whether it's a gap in the market, a new customer need, or an emerging trend, the first step in making the case for innovation is identifying the opportunity it addresses. The business case should outline the market potential and demonstrate how innovation aligns with consumer demands or industry shifts.

PIVOT MAGAZINE | March 2025

2. Competitive Advantage:
Innovation often provides companies with a competitive edge, whether it's through product differentiation, improved customer experiences, or cost reductions. A solid business case will highlight how innovation can help the company gain a sustainable competitive advantage and position itself as a leader in its field.

3. Financial Impact: Financial projections are critical when building a business case for innovation. These projections should not only include expected revenue growth but also account for costs, resource allocation, and potential risks. A well-rounded business case will demonstrate how the innovation will contribute to the company's bottom line, while factoring in the investments needed for development, implementation, and scaling.

4. Legal and Ethical
Considerations: Beyond financial metrics, innovation must be evaluated through a legal and ethical lens. Businesses must ensure that their innovations do not violate laws or ethical principles, particularly in industries like healthcare, finance, and technology, where regulatory oversight is high. Ethical considerations, such as data privacy, environmental impact, and social responsibility, must be carefully integrated into the business case.

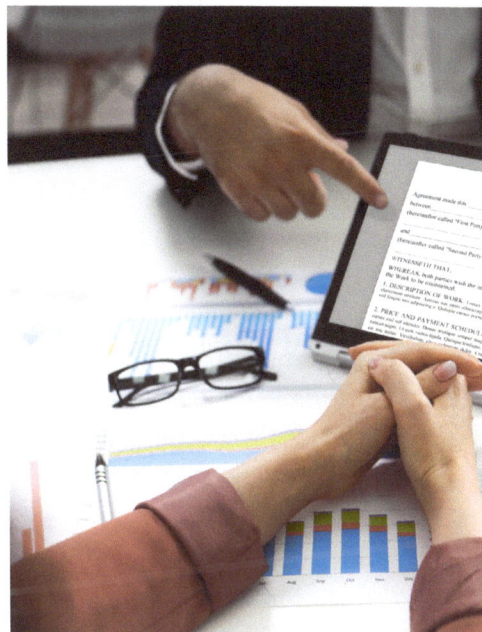

Legal Boundaries of Innovation: What to Watch Out For

The legal landscape surrounding innovation is complex and constantly evolving. As businesses develop new products or services, they must navigate a range of legal issues, including intellectual property rights, product safety regulations, data privacy laws, and environmental standards.

1. Intellectual Property (IP) Protection: One of the first legal considerations for companies pursuing innovation is intellectual property. Intellectual property includes patents, trademarks, copyrights, and trade secrets, all of which help protect a company's ideas and innovations from being copied or used without permission.

When developing a new product or service, companies must consider how to protect their intellectual property. This may involve filing for patents to safeguard technological innovations, trademarking brand names, or securing copyright protection for creative works. Failure to properly protect intellectual property can result in competitors copying the product, undermining the business's competitive advantage.

Case Study: Apple has long been an innovator in the tech industry, consistently introducing new products like the iPhone, iPad, and Apple Watch. A significant part of Apple's success can be attributed to its strong intellectual property protections. For example, Apple has filed thousands of patents over the years, ensuring that its products are protected from imitation by competitors.

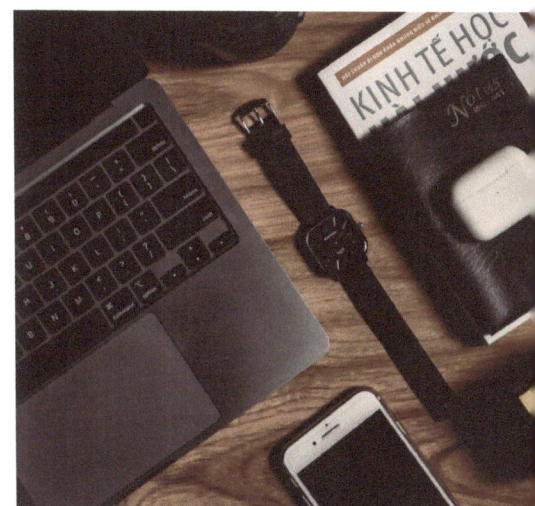

In contrast, companies that fail to secure IP protection risk losing their innovations to copycat businesses.

2. Product Safety and Compliance: In regulated industries such as healthcare, pharmaceuticals, automotive, and consumer goods, product safety and compliance are crucial. Innovation must not come at the expense of safety, and businesses must ensure that new products meet all relevant safety standards and regulations.

For example, a tech company developing new consumer electronics must comply with safety standards related to electrical components, battery safety, and environmental impact. Failure to meet these standards can result in costly recalls, legal action, and reputational damage.

Case Study: The automotive industry has faced numerous legal challenges regarding product safety in recent years. For instance, in 2015, Volkswagen was involved in a massive emissions scandal, where the company had installed software in diesel vehicles to cheat emissions tests. The legal and financial fallout from this innovation, designed to make cars appear more eco-friendly than they were, was immense. Volkswagen faced billions in fines and a loss of consumer trust. This case underscores the importance of ensuring that innovations comply with safety and regulatory standards.

3. Data Privacy and Protection: In today's digital age, data privacy is a critical concern for businesses that rely on customer data to drive innovation. Whether it's using data for personalized marketing, AI-driven recommendations, or product development, companies must ensure that they are compliant with data privacy laws.

Laws such as the European Union's General Data Protection Regulation (GDPR) and the California Consumer Privacy Act (CCPA) impose strict requirements on how businesses collect, store, and use personal data. Innovation that involves customer data must be designed with these legal frameworks in mind to avoid penalties and protect consumer privacy.

Example: A leading e-commerce platform recently introduced an AI-powered recommendation engine that used customer purchase data to suggest products. However, after the implementation, the company was fined for not properly informing customers about how their data would be used. This highlighted the importance of ensuring that innovation does not compromise data privacy or violate privacy laws.

Ethical Boundaries of Innovation: A Corporate Responsibility

While legal considerations ensure compliance with regulations, ethical considerations help ensure that innovation aligns with societal values and does not exploit vulnerable populations or harm the environment. Ethical innovation is about creating value not only for the business but for the broader community and future generations.

1. Environmental Impact: As companies innovate, they must consider the environmental impact of their products, processes, and technologies. This includes evaluating the carbon footprint, resource consumption, waste management, and sustainability of new products or services. Innovating without considering environmental consequences can lead to harmful practices and long-term damage to the planet, which may, in turn, damage a company's reputation and consumer trust.

Case Study: Tesla has revolutionized the automotive industry with its electric vehicles. Beyond the financial benefits of offering eco-friendly alternatives to traditional gasoline-powered cars, Tesla's innovations align with the company's commitment to sustainability. Tesla not only creates electric vehicles but also focuses on energy storage and solar energy solutions, helping reduce dependence on fossil fuels.

However, even with such innovations, Tesla must continually ensure that its production processes are environmentally responsible. The mining of materials for batteries, for example, has raised concerns about environmental degradation and worker safety. Companies like Tesla are now focusing on sustainable practices throughout their supply chain to maintain their reputation as leaders in ethical innovation.

2. Social Responsibility: Ethical innovation also requires businesses to consider the social implications of their products and services. This includes assessing whether innovations will contribute positively to society, or whether they may perpetuate inequality, cause harm, or exploit vulnerable populations.

For example, the rise of social media platforms has brought tremendous benefits, allowing businesses to connect with consumers in real-time. However, these innovations have also led to concerns about data manipulation, privacy violations, and mental health issues. Ethical innovators must consider the broader social impact of their products, particularly when creating platforms that influence public opinion or consumer behavior.

Example: In 2018, Facebook faced backlash over the Cambridge Analytica scandal, where personal data of millions of users was harvested without consent and used for political targeting. The company was accused of enabling unethical data practices that violated consumer privacy. This case highlights the importance of ethical leadership in the tech industry and the need for responsible innovation that prioritizes the welfare of users.

3. Ethical Labor Practices: Innovation also has ethical implications regarding labor practices. Companies developing new technologies or products must ensure that they do not exploit workers, particularly in developing countries where labor laws may be lax or unenforced. Ethical businesses should commit to fair wages, safe working conditions, and respect for workers' rights, even when producing goods in lower-cost markets.

Case Study: Apple's supply chain has been scrutinized for its labor practices in countries like China, where some of its manufacturing partners have been accused of poor working conditions and low wages. In response, Apple has taken steps to improve labor standards and transparency in its supply chain, ensuring that all suppliers comply with the company's strict codes of conduct.

Navigating Legal and Ethical Innovation in a Global Marketplace

One of the biggest challenges companies face in building a business case for innovation is the global nature of today's markets. While laws and ethical standards may differ between countries, companies must navigate these differences while maintaining a consistent commitment to legal and ethical principles.

Global Legal Compliance

For businesses operating in multiple countries, it's essential to understand the varying legal frameworks that govern innovation. While some regulations, like those surrounding intellectual property or product safety, may be universal, others—such as labor laws, environmental standards, and data privacy rules—can differ greatly between regions.

Example: A company that operates in both the U.S. and the European Union must comply with GDPR in Europe, which imposes strict data privacy requirements, while simultaneously adhering to U.S. privacy laws that may be more lenient. Navigating these different requirements can be complex, but failing to comply with regulations in any jurisdiction can result in penalties and legal challenges.

Cultural Sensitivity and Ethical Innovation

Innovation is not only about complying with legal standards but also understanding the cultural context in which a product or service will be used.

Ethical innovation involves ensuring that new products are respectful of cultural norms and values, especially when operating in international markets.

For example, a fashion company that introduces a new clothing line may need to consider cultural sensitivities in different regions. What may be considered fashionable or acceptable in one market could be deemed offensive or inappropriate in another. Ethical leaders ensure that innovations are developed with a global perspective in mind, respecting local customs and traditions.

Conclusion: The Future of Ethical and Legal Innovation

In conclusion, building a business case for innovation that is both legally sound and ethically responsible is not just about avoiding risks—it is about creating sustainable value.

Companies that prioritize both innovation and ethics are better positioned to succeed in today's rapidly evolving business environment. By aligning innovation with legal compliance and social responsibility, businesses can ensure that their growth is not only profitable but also positive for society and the planet.

As the world continues to evolve, the companies that lead the way in ethical innovation will be the ones that not only thrive financially but also contribute to a better and more sustainable future. The road to successful innovation may be challenging, but with careful planning, legal foresight, and a commitment to ethics, businesses can create lasting value for all stakeholders involved.

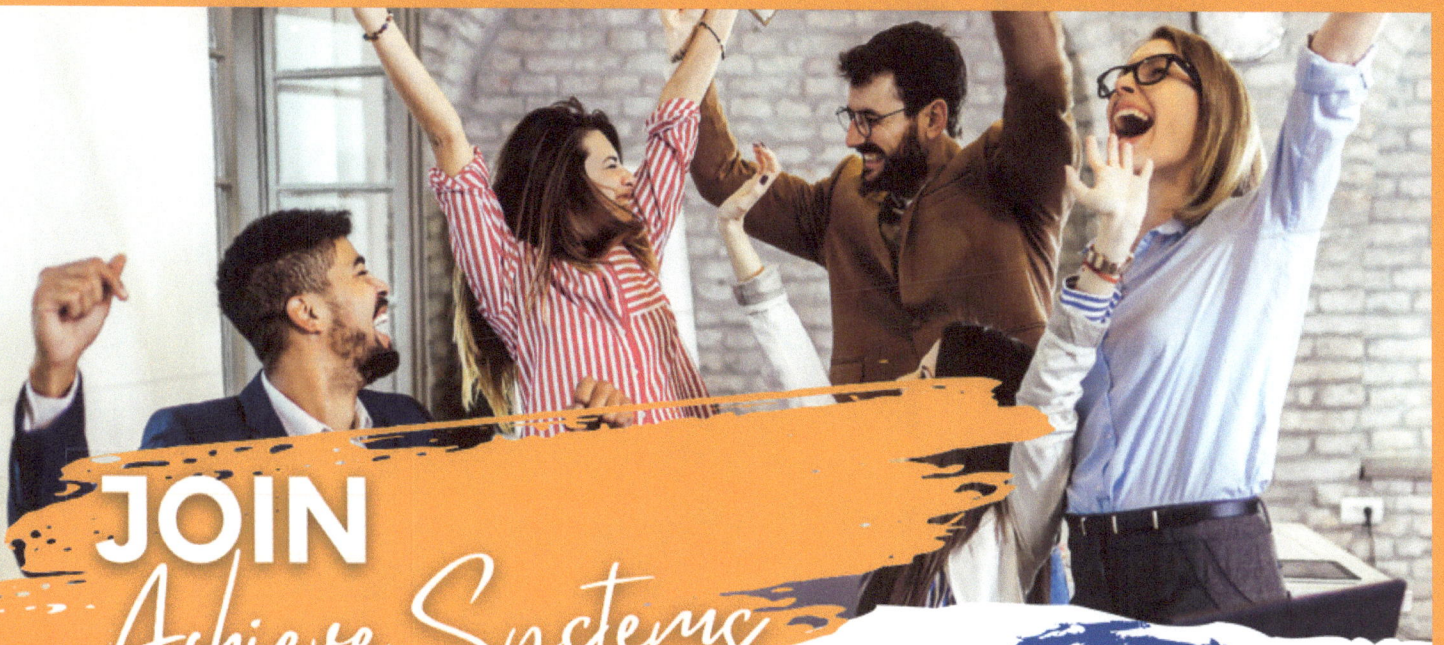

JOIN
Achieve Systems

BECOME AN ACHIEVE SYSTEMS MEMBER TODAY!

Education
We help you get the tools to create a thriving business! It's turnkey, you can start NOW!

Marketing
We provide marketing guidelines but also plug you into our conferences, events and database

Community
We have a thriving community of entrepreneurs and business owners for you to collaborate, refer and partner with to grow and up-level your business!

WE WORK WITH ENTREPRENEURS, BUSINESS OWNERS, SPEAKERS & LEADERS!

CONTACT US OR REGISTER HERE: www.AchieveSystemsPro.com

Organizational Overhaul: Strategies for Improving Your Company Culture

In today's rapidly changing business environment, organizations must continually evolve to remain competitive, relevant, and resilient. One of the most critical components of this evolution is the culture within the organization. Company culture is the foundation on which all business activities—be it innovation, customer service, or employee retention—are built. A positive, inclusive, and high-performing culture can be a powerful catalyst for success, while a toxic or misaligned culture can undermine even the most promising business strategies.

An organizational overhaul aimed at improving company culture is not just about enhancing employee satisfaction or improving workplace aesthetics. It involves rethinking core values, aligning leadership with organizational goals, and implementing strategic initiatives that drive engagement, accountability, and performance. This process is critical not only for fostering a positive work environment but also for ensuring that the organization can thrive in an increasingly complex and competitive business landscape.

This article explores the importance of organizational culture, provides actionable strategies for improving it, and examines the legal, ethical, and practical considerations that companies must address during a culture transformation.

Why Company Culture Matters

The culture within an organization defines how its employees interact with one another, how they approach their work, and how they relate to customers, suppliers, and stakeholders. Culture shapes everything from decision-making processes and communication styles to how employees feel about their work and their level of engagement.

1. Attracting and Retaining Top Talent: In a tight labor market, company culture can make or break an organization's ability to attract and retain top talent. A positive, inclusive culture fosters an environment where employees feel valued, respected, and empowered to do their best work. This, in turn, leads to higher levels of employee satisfaction, loyalty, and retention.

On the other hand, a toxic or disengaged culture can drive employees away, leading to high turnover rates and the loss of valuable skills and expertise. Companies that prioritize culture often have a significant competitive advantage when it comes to talent acquisition, as top candidates actively seek workplaces where they will feel supported and motivated.

Case Study: Google is widely known for its innovative and employee-centric culture. The company provides flexible work schedules, career development opportunities, and a collaborative environment that encourages creativity and open communication. Google's culture is a key factor in its ability to attract and retain top talent, which has helped the company remain a leader in the tech industry.

2. Improving Employee:

Engagement and Productivity An aligned company culture leads to better employee engagement, which is directly correlated with increased productivity. Employees who are engaged are more likely to go above and beyond their job descriptions, contribute ideas, and collaborate with colleagues. They are also more likely to stay with the company, reducing turnover costs and improving team dynamics.

Research consistently shows that engaged employees are more productive, more creative, and more committed to achieving organizational goals. They are also more likely to provide excellent customer service, which can result in improved customer satisfaction and business performance.

3. Strengthening Organizational Resilience: In a

business environment marked by uncertainty, economic shifts, and constant change, organizational culture is essential for building resilience. A strong, adaptable culture helps companies navigate challenges by fostering open communication, encouraging innovation, and promoting collaboration.

When employees feel connected to the company's values and mission, they are more likely to contribute to

problem-solving during tough times. Organizational culture becomes a vital tool for ensuring that employees remain committed, motivated, and proactive when the company faces adversity.

4. Enhancing Customer Experience: A company's culture often directly impacts how it interacts with customers. Companies that prioritize culture and employee satisfaction tend to have employees who are more engaged with customers, more willing to go the extra mile, and more focused on delivering excellent service. The result is a stronger, more consistent customer experience.

Case Study: Zappos, the online retailer known for its exceptional customer service, has built its reputation on a strong, customer-first culture. The company empowers its employees to take the time necessary to resolve customer issues and exceed expectations. Zappos has consistently been recognized for its outstanding customer service, which is rooted in its company culture of customer-centricity and employee empowerment.

Key Strategies for Improving Company Culture

Improving company culture requires a strategic, thoughtful approach. It is not something that can be achieved overnight, but with the right focus and commitment from leadership, significant positive change can be made. Below are key strategies for transforming and improving your organization's culture.

1. Leadership Alignment and Commitment:

Company culture starts at the top. Leaders play a critical role in shaping the organizational culture, and their actions, attitudes, and behaviors set the tone for the entire company. To drive a successful culture transformation, leadership must be fully aligned with the cultural shift and committed to modeling the desired values and behaviors.

Leaders must be willing to communicate openly, listen to feedback, and be transparent about their intentions. They must also be prepared to lead by example, demonstrating the behaviors and values they expect from their employees.

Actionable Steps:

- Host regular leadership meetings to discuss culture and the changes needed.
- Provide leadership development programs that focus on emotional intelligence, communication, and ethical decision-making.
- Hold leaders accountable for fostering a positive culture by incorporating cultural metrics into performance evaluations.

2. Defining and Communicating Core Values:

A strong company culture is built upon clearly defined core values. These values should reflect the company's mission, vision, and long-term goals, and they should serve as a guide for decision-making at all levels of the organization. By communicating these values consistently and ensuring that they are reinforced through company policies, employee training, and leadership behavior, organizations can create a shared sense of purpose and direction.

Actionable Steps:

- Engage employees in defining the company's core values, ensuring that they are meaningful and relevant.
- Create a values-based decision-making framework that employees can refer to when faced with tough choices.
- Regularly reinforce core values through internal communications, team-building activities, and recognition programs.

3. Fostering Open Communication and Transparency:

Transparency is one of the cornerstones of a healthy organizational culture. Employees need to feel that they are part of an open, honest dialogue with leadership and that their opinions are valued. Open communication helps prevent misunderstandings, build trust, and ensure that everyone is aligned with the organization's goals.

Actionable Steps:

- Implement regular town hall meetings, where employees can ask questions and engage with leadership.
- Use internal communications platforms to share updates on company performance, cultural initiatives, and employee achievements.
- Encourage a feedback loop, where employees can voice concerns or suggestions without fear of retaliation.

4. Promoting Diversity and Inclusion. Diversity and inclusion (D&I) are integral components of a strong company culture. An inclusive culture fosters a sense of belonging, which can lead to increased employee engagement, satisfaction, and retention. Embracing diversity in all its forms—including race, gender, age, and background—ensures that the company benefits from a wide range of perspectives and ideas.

Case Study: Salesforce, a global cloud-based software company, has made diversity and inclusion a central part of its corporate culture. Through its "Ohana" (family) culture, Salesforce emphasizes inclusivity, employee support, and community building. The company has also implemented programs to ensure equal pay and provide equal opportunities for all employees, regardless of gender or ethnicity.

Actionable Steps:

- Create D&I training programs to educate employees about unconscious bias and inclusivity.
- Establish mentorship programs that pair underrepresented employees with senior leaders.
- Regularly assess the diversity of your workforce and take action to improve inclusion at all levels.

5. Empowering Employees and Encouraging Autonomy: A key component of improving company culture is empowering employees to take ownership of their work and encouraging autonomy. When employees feel trusted and empowered, they are more likely to be engaged and motivated to contribute to the company's success.

Actionable Steps:

- Give employees more control over their work by allowing them to set their own goals and schedules.
- Encourage collaboration and innovation by creating cross-functional teams that allow employees to work on projects outside their immediate roles.
- Provide employees with the tools and resources they need to succeed and grow in their careers.

Legal and Ethical Considerations in Cultural Transformation

When undergoing an organizational overhaul, it is essential to keep legal and ethical considerations in mind. Organizational culture changes may involve adjustments to policies, recruitment practices, compensation, and performance management, all of which must comply with applicable laws and regulations.

1. Compliance with Employment Laws: Any cultural shift that involves changes to employee behavior, compensation, or benefits must comply with labor laws and regulations. These include laws regarding fair treatment, discrimination, and harassment, as well as wage and hour laws.

2. Ethical Labor Practices: When improving company culture, it is vital to ensure that the company treats all employees ethically and equitably. This means ensuring fair pay, providing a safe working environment, and offering equal opportunities for advancement.

Conclusion

Organizational overhauls aimed at improving company culture are essential for creating a thriving, resilient, and engaged workforce. By aligning leadership with company values, fostering diversity and inclusion, encouraging transparency, and empowering employees, businesses can transform their culture and unlock long-term success.

As companies undergo this transformation, it's essential to remain mindful of the legal and ethical considerations that impact culture change. Prioritizing compliance, fair treatment, and ethical leadership ensures that the company can make the most of its cultural transformation while mitigating risks.

The road to a positive, productive, and sustainable company culture is not easy, but with the right strategies, commitment, and leadership, organizations can create a culture that fosters innovation, collaboration, and growth.

MICROCASTING

Supercharge Your Business!

Do you want to find new ways to add additional income to your coaching, consulting, or content creation business?

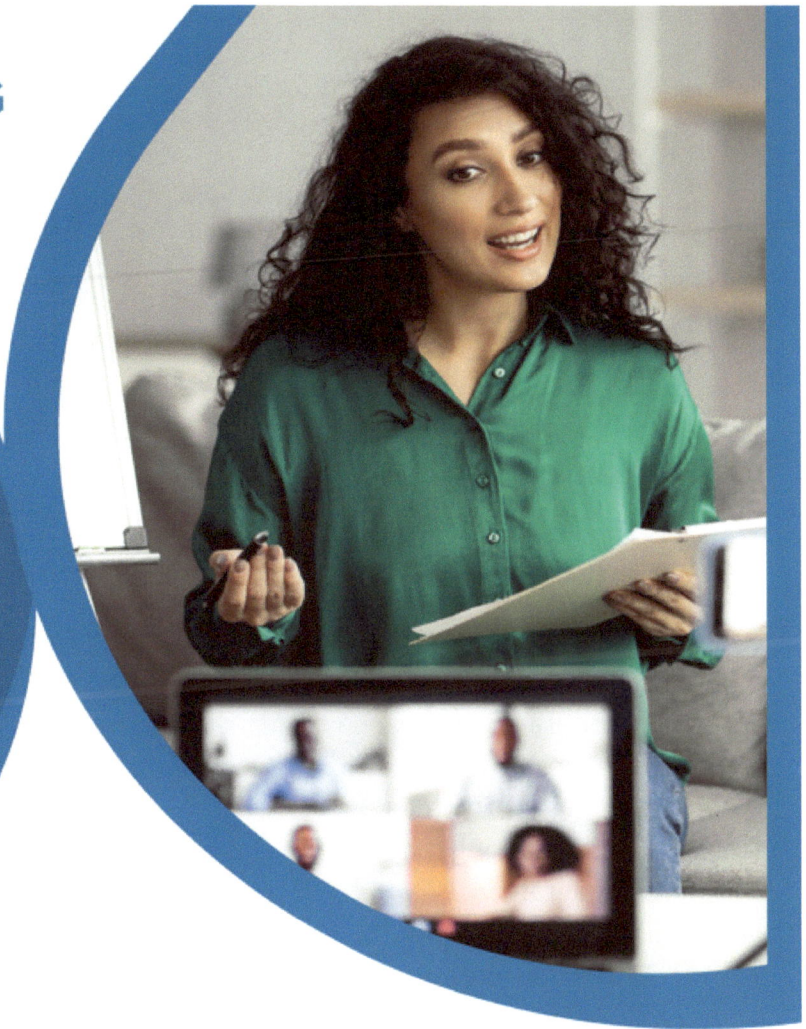

eLearning Portals by Microcasting is specifically designed for Coaches, Consultants, and Course Creators to engage your customers, establish yourself as a thought leader, and grow your revenues.

Here are just a few things you can do with **Microcasting**:

- ⊘ **Start selling** your courses and programs.
- ⊘ Create a **paid membership site** to grow your revenues.
- ⊘ Build a free membership site to **increase lead gen**.
- ⊘ Easily **integrate eLearning** into your marketing website.
- ⊘ Create **individualized customer portals** .
- ⊘ And so much more...

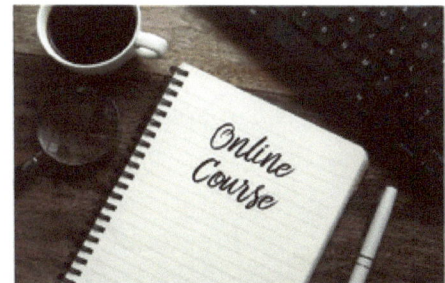

Microcasting is an all-in-one online learning platform that makes it easy for course creators to design, manage, and market their courses. With its personalized eLearning experience, you can keep your current customers engaged with your business, generating more upsells and higher renewal rates. Create courses quickly and effortlessly - all with the help of Microcasting!

Try Microcasting today and start transforming your business!

Request a demo - email us at ✉ info@microcasting.com **OR VISIT** 🌐 www.elearning-portals.com

The Role of Corporate Governance in Legal Risk Mitigation

In today's fast-paced business environment, companies face a multitude of legal risks, ranging from regulatory compliance issues to potential lawsuits, data privacy concerns, and environmental obligations. Effective corporate governance is one of the most critical elements for mitigating these legal risks and ensuring that businesses operate in a responsible and compliant manner. Strong corporate governance structures help organizations navigate complex legal frameworks, make informed decisions, and protect themselves from legal pitfalls.

Corporate governance refers to the systems, processes, and practices that guide how a company is directed, managed, and controlled. It involves the relationships between the company's board of directors, management, shareholders, and other stakeholders. Governance structures are designed to ensure transparency, accountability, and fairness in business operations, all of which are essential for reducing legal exposure and enhancing business resilience.

This article will explore the essential role corporate governance plays in legal risk mitigation, detailing the importance of proper governance frameworks, best practices, and the legal implications of failing to prioritize governance. It will also provide practical advice for building a robust governance system and maintaining legal compliance, using real-world case studies to highlight both successes and failures.

The Basics of Corporate Governance

Corporate governance consists of a set of rules and processes that define the relationships between a company's management, its board of directors, and its shareholders. The primary goal of corporate governance is to ensure that companies are run in a manner that maximizes shareholder value, while also considering the interests of other stakeholders such as employees, customers, and the community. Effective governance ensures that decisions are made with integrity and in compliance with applicable laws, which can significantly reduce legal and financial risks.

Key Components of Corporate Governance

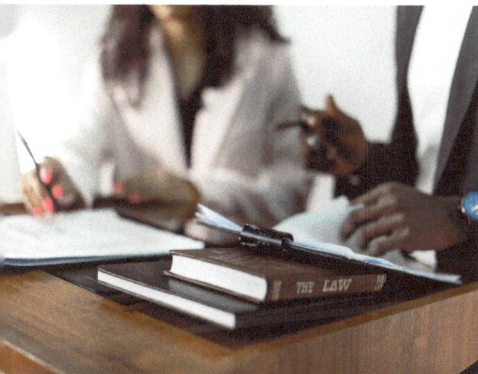

1. **Board of Directors:** The board is responsible for overseeing the company's strategic direction, risk management, and overall operations. It is the board's duty to ensure that the company is managed in a way that aligns with shareholder interests and complies with legal and regulatory standards. Board members must have the expertise, independence, and commitment to fulfill their roles effectively.

2. **Management:** While the board provides oversight, management is responsible for the day-to-day operations of the company. Good governance ensures that management operates transparently, ethically, and within the boundaries of the law, while reporting to the board on financial performance, legal risks, and strategic initiatives.

3. **Shareholders and Stakeholders:** Governance frameworks should balance the interests of shareholders and other stakeholders. Engaging with stakeholders in a meaningful way—whether through annual general meetings, surveys, or regular updates—helps ensure transparency and builds trust.

4. **Internal Controls and Compliance:** One of the cornerstones of corporate governance is the implementation of internal controls designed to prevent legal violations and mitigate risks. These controls can include audit committees, compliance officers, and reporting systems that ensure the organization adheres to laws and regulations.

Legal Risks That Corporate Governance Can Mitigate

There are a variety of legal risks that organizations must address to ensure their long-term sustainability. Corporate governance plays a central role in identifying, managing, and mitigating these risks, ensuring that companies avoid litigation, fines, and reputational damage.

1. Regulatory Compliance Risks: Regulatory compliance is perhaps the most significant legal risk that companies face

Companies must comply with industry-specific regulations, such as the Sarbanes-Oxley Act (SOX) for financial reporting in the United States, the General Data Protection Regulation (GDPR) in Europe for data privacy, and environmental laws governing emissions and waste disposal.

Case Study: In 2008, the financial services industry was rocked by a massive scandal involving the misreporting of financial data. Major companies, including Enron and WorldCom, faced significant legal consequences for failing to adhere to financial reporting and auditing regulations. The aftermath of these scandals led to stricter regulatory requirements, such as the SOX Act, which significantly impacted corporate governance structures in publicly traded companies.

With proper governance, businesses can better ensure compliance with regulatory requirements, reduce exposure to potential fines or penalties, and enhance their credibility with stakeholders.

2. Legal Risks Associated with Contracts and Agreements:

Businesses often face legal risks related to contracts, including breaches of contract, disputes over terms, or failure to fulfill obligations. Effective governance ensures that businesses have robust contract management systems in place, including proper review processes, clear agreements, and dispute resolution mechanisms.

A board that is well-versed in contract law and ensures appropriate oversight of significant business agreements can prevent costly litigation and reputational damage.

Example: A tech company that failed to ensure adequate legal review of a licensing agreement for proprietary software may find itself embroiled in a legal dispute over intellectual property rights. By instituting robust governance practices, such as having a legal team review all high-risk contracts, companies can avoid these kinds of costly pitfalls.

3. Risk Management and Corporate Liability:

One of the most important roles of corporate governance is risk management. Boards are responsible for ensuring that businesses have adequate risk management frameworks in place to identify potential legal risks and take steps to mitigate them. This includes managing risks related to product liability, employee safety, environmental hazards, and cybersecurity.

Effective risk management includes maintaining insurance coverage, ensuring health and safety standards, and putting systems in place to detect and prevent fraud or other forms of corporate misconduct.

Case Study: In the early 2000s, BP faced significant legal and financial repercussions following the Deepwater Horizon oil spill in the Gulf of Mexico. The company was held liable for violating environmental regulations, and its governance practices came under intense scrutiny. BP's inability to properly address environmental risks and put in place adequate safety controls led to massive fines, legal settlements, and a tarnished reputation.

Best Practices for Corporate Governance and Legal Risk Mitigation

The best corporate governance practices help ensure that organizations maintain legal compliance, minimize risk, and operate with integrity. Below are some key practices that can strengthen corporate governance and reduce legal risks.

1. Establishing Clear Policies and Procedures:

A critical component of good corporate governance is having well-defined policies and procedures in place. These policies should address key areas such as ethics, compliance, risk management, and corporate responsibility. Clear policies ensure that all employees understand their roles, responsibilities, and the company's expectations.

Actionable Step: Regularly review and update company policies to ensure they comply with new regulations. This includes reviewing internal controls, code of conduct, conflict-of-interest policies, and data protection measures.

2. Promoting Board Independence and Diversity:

Board independence is crucial for effective governance.

Independent board members can provide objective oversight, challenge management decisions, and ensure that the interests of shareholders and stakeholders are being adequately represented. Furthermore, having a diverse board helps bring a range of perspectives, which is essential for making informed and responsible decisions.

Actionable Step: Companies should periodically assess their board composition and ensure that it reflects a diversity of experiences, backgrounds, and expertise.

3. Regular Audits and Compliance Reviews:
One of the most effective ways to mitigate legal risks is through regular internal audits and compliance reviews. These reviews ensure that the company is adhering to regulatory standards, identify areas of improvement, and provide assurance to stakeholders that the business is operating ethically and legally.

Actionable Step: Conduct internal audits at least annually to review financial statements, compliance with regulatory requirements, and adherence to company policies. Third-party audits can also provide an objective evaluation of governance practices.

4. Strengthening Ethical Decision-Making :
Corporate governance should foster ethical decision-making at all levels of the organization. Ethical leadership involves modeling the right behavior, making decisions that prioritize long-term value, and promoting a culture where integrity is valued. Board members and senior executives should lead by example, setting the tone for the rest of the organization.

Actionable Step: Implement ethics training programs for all employees, and develop mechanisms for reporting unethical behavior. Senior leaders should actively engage in the ethical training process to reinforce the company's commitment to integrity.

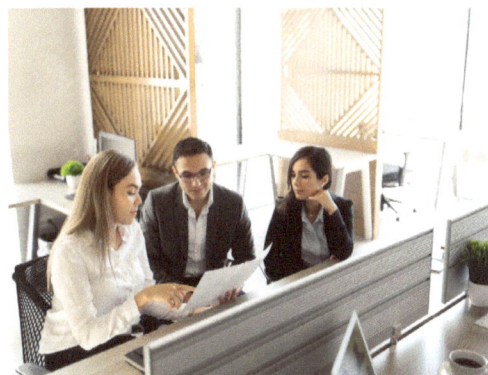

Legal Considerations in Corporate Governance

In addition to best practices, there are specific legal considerations that businesses must keep in mind when designing and maintaining their corporate governance frameworks.

1. Fiduciary Duties of Directors:
Directors of a company have fiduciary duties to act in the best interest of the shareholders and the company. This includes the duty of care, the duty of loyalty, and the duty of good faith. A failure to uphold these duties can expose the company to legal liability.

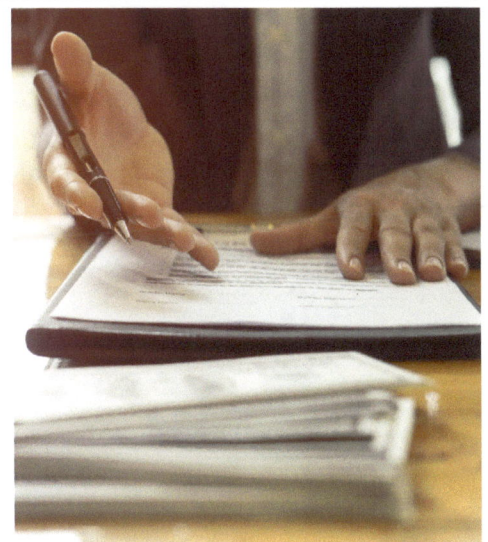

Case Study: In 2001, the board of Enron failed to properly oversee the company's financial dealings, leading to the company's collapse. The board's failure to act in the best interests of shareholders and to ensure financial transparency was a major factor in the legal fallout from Enron's bankruptcy.

2. Shareholder Rights and Governance:
Companies must also respect shareholders' rights in their governance practices. This includes providing shareholders with voting rights, access to information, and the ability to raise concerns about management practices. Shareholder activism has increased in recent years, with investors taking a more active role in influencing corporate governance decisions.

Actionable Step: Regularly engage with shareholders and ensure they have access to relevant information, such as financial statements, governance policies, and the company's strategic direction. This helps build trust and transparency in corporate governance.

In conclusion, corporate governance is a critical mechanism for mitigating legal risks and ensuring that businesses operate ethically and within the boundaries of the law. By implementing best practices, establishing strong oversight, and prioritizing legal and ethical considerations, businesses can not only reduce their exposure to legal liabilities but also build a more resilient and transparent organization.

As the business environment becomes increasingly complex, effective corporate governance will continue to be a key factor in navigating legal risks and ensuring long-term success. Companies that embrace strong governance practices will be better positioned to handle challenges, maintain stakeholder trust, and foster a culture of integrity.

Mastering Crisis Management: A Roadmap to Resilience

In the unpredictable world of business, crises are inevitable. Whether it's an economic downturn, a natural disaster, a product recall, or a public relations disaster, organizations must be prepared to navigate the turbulence of a crisis and emerge stronger. The ability to effectively manage crises is what differentiates resilient companies from those that falter in the face of adversity.

Crisis management is not just about reacting to an emergency when it strikes; it's about creating a robust plan, building an agile team, and ensuring that the company can weather the storm without significant long-term damage. Mastering crisis management requires strategic foresight, communication skills, and a focus on long-term resilience.

This article will provide a roadmap to mastering crisis management, offering strategies and frameworks to help businesses respond to crises with agility, transparency, and accountability. Through real-world examples and actionable insights, we will explore how companies can prepare for the worst, mitigate risks, and emerge stronger from challenging situations.

Understanding Crisis Management

Crisis management is the process by which an organization handles a disruptive event that threatens to harm its reputation, operations, financial stability, or overall ability to function. A crisis can come in many forms, and its impact can vary depending on the nature of the organization and its preparedness. The key to successful crisis management is not just surviving the event but also maintaining trust, minimizing harm, and positioning the organization for recovery.

Types of Crises

- **Natural Disasters:** These include hurricanes, earthquakes, floods, fires, and pandemics. Such crises often disrupt operations, affect the workforce, and can have long-lasting economic effects.

- **Product Failures or Recalls:** A product defect that causes harm to consumers can severely damage a company's reputation and lead to legal consequences. For example, a food product recall due to contamination can lead to loss of consumer trust and market share.
- **Financial Crises:** These can be caused by economic downturns, cash flow problems, or financial mismanagement. The collapse of a financial institution or a company's sudden insolvency is often due to poor financial crisis management.
- **Public Relations (PR) Crises:** These involve scandals or negative publicity that can harm an organization's reputation. For example, a controversial comment from a CEO or a brand misstep in the public eye can result in public backlash.
- **Cybersecurity Breaches:** With the rise of technology, businesses face a growing threat of cyberattacks, which can compromise sensitive customer data, disrupt operations, and damage a company's reputation.
- **Legal and Ethical Crises:** These occur when a company faces legal action or is involved in a scandal related to unethical practices. For example, fraud, discrimination, or violation of environmental regulations can lead to legal battles and reputational damage.

The Impact of Crises on Organizations

The impact of crises can be wide-ranging, touching every facet of the business. Some common consequences include:

- **Reputation Damage:** A crisis often leads to negative publicity, which can tarnish a company's brand image and diminish customer trust.
- **Financial Losses:** Direct costs associated with managing the crisis, as well as long-term losses from disrupted operations or declining sales, can severely affect a company's bottom line.
- **Employee Morale:** During a crisis, employees may feel insecure, leading to lower productivity, increased turnover, and difficulties in maintaining operations.
- **Legal and Regulatory Challenges:** Depending on the nature of the crisis, businesses may face legal penalties, regulatory scrutiny, and lawsuits.
- **Disrupted Operations:** In some cases, a crisis can disrupt day-to-day operations, making it difficult for the business to function normally. This can include supply chain issues, damaged infrastructure, or the inability to maintain customer service standards.

The Importance of Crisis Management Planning

A well-crafted crisis management plan (CMP) is a critical tool for ensuring that an organization is prepared to respond swiftly and effectively. Crisis management planning is not about predicting every possible crisis; instead, it's about being prepared for any eventuality by having a clear, flexible framework in place.

The Key Components of a Crisis Management Plan

1. **Crisis Team Formation:** Designate a crisis management team (CMT) that will be responsible for handling the situation. This team should include representatives from leadership, communications, legal, HR, operations, and other relevant departments. Having a diverse team ensures that all aspects of the crisis are addressed.
2. **Risk Assessment and Identification:** Identify potential risks and assess their impact on the organization. This includes understanding the

likelihood of each type of crisis, its potential impact, and the organization's capacity to mitigate it.

3. Clear Communication Channels: A key part of crisis management is ensuring that there is clear, transparent communication with all stakeholders—employees, customers, suppliers, regulators, and the media. Having a well-defined communication strategy helps prevent confusion and misinformation during a crisis.

4. Resource Allocation: Determine the resources—financial, human, and technological—that will be needed to manage the crisis. Ensure that these resources are readily available and can be quickly mobilized when needed.

5. Post-Crisis Recovery Plan: Once the crisis has passed, focus on recovery and rebuilding. This includes assessing the damage, repairing relationships with stakeholders, restoring operations, and learning from the crisis to prevent future occurrences.

Building Organizational Resilience

While crisis management focuses on the immediate response, organizational resilience is about preparing the company to withstand and adapt to disruptions over the long term. Resilience is built on a foundation of proactive strategies, strong leadership, and a culture of agility.

1. Strengthening Leadership and Decision-Making: Strong, decisive leadership is crucial during a crisis. Leaders must be able to make tough decisions quickly, remain calm under pressure, and inspire confidence in their teams. A resilient organization has leadership that is equipped with the skills and mindset to navigate uncertainty.

Actionable Step: Invest in leadership development programs that focus on crisis management, decision-making under pressure, and emotional intelligence. Equip leaders with the tools to guide their teams through challenging times.

2. Developing a Culture of Agility and Adaptability: In a resilient organization, employees are empowered to adapt and respond to change. This means fostering a culture where innovation is encouraged, risks are managed, and change is embraced. Agility ensures that the organization can pivot quickly in response to crises, whether it's shifting operations, adjusting business models, or rethinking marketing strategies.

Actionable Step: Encourage continuous learning and foster a growth mindset across the organization. Provide employees with the resources and training to think critically, solve problems, and collaborate effectively during a crisis.

3. Investing in Technology and Infrastructure: In today's world, technology is a key enabler of resilience. Businesses that invest in robust IT systems, data protection, and cybersecurity measures are better equipped to handle crises, particularly those involving data breaches or cyberattacks. Resilient organizations also have backup systems in place to ensure business continuity during disruptions.

Case Study: During the COVID-19 pandemic, companies that had already implemented digital tools and remote work infrastructure were able to continue operations with minimal disruption. Businesses that hadn't embraced technology found it much harder to pivot and maintain operations during the global lockdown.

Actionable Step: Invest in cloud solutions, backup systems, and cybersecurity infrastructure. Ensure that remote work capabilities are in place so that employees can work effectively even during physical disruptions.

4. Fostering Communication and Collaboration: In times of crisis, effective communication is the key to success. Resilient organizations prioritize open communication channels and ensure that information is shared efficiently and transparently across all levels of the company. Collaboration also plays a vital role, as cross-functional teams must work together to respond to crises quickly and effectively.

Actionable Step: Implement collaborative platforms (such as Slack, Microsoft Teams, or Zoom) to ensure that teams can communicate in real time during a crisis. Train employees in crisis communication protocols, so everyone knows how to act and whom to contact during an emergency.

Real-World Crisis Management Case Studies

1. Johnson & Johnson's Tylenol Crisis (1982): One of the most well-known examples of successful crisis management is Johnson & Johnson's handling of the Tylenol poisonings in 1982. When seven people in the Chicago area died after taking Tylenol capsules laced with cyanide, the company immediately recalled 31 million bottles of the product, despite the significant financial loss it would incur. The company's commitment to customer safety and transparency earned it widespread praise and restored its reputation.

This crisis showed the importance of swift action, transparency, and prioritizing consumer trust over short-term profits.

2. Toyota's Recall Crisis (2009-2010): In 2009, Toyota faced a massive recall crisis after defects in its vehicles were linked to sudden acceleration accidents. The company initially struggled with its response, delaying its recall and offering unclear communication. However, after leadership changes and improved communication, Toyota eventually regained consumer trust by taking responsibility, improving its quality control systems, and launching a comprehensive customer safety campaign.

This crisis highlights the importance of leadership accountability and the need for continuous improvement in product quality and safety.

3. BP's Deepwater Horizon Oil Spill (2010): BP's handling of the Deepwater Horizon oil spill is often cited as an example of poor crisis management. The company's slow response, lack of transparency, and failure to take immediate responsibility led to significant legal, financial, and reputational consequences. The crisis ultimately cost BP billions in fines, settlements, and damage to its reputation.

This case underscores the importance of transparency, accountability, and swift action in crisis management. BP's failure to adequately address the crisis early on contributed to its long-term struggles.

In conclusion, mastering crisis management is essential for any business that wants to thrive in today's unpredictable world. By developing a comprehensive crisis management plan, building organizational resilience, and learning from past crises, businesses can improve their ability to respond to disruptions quickly and effectively. Companies that are prepared for crises are better equipped to maintain operations, protect their reputation, and minimize financial losses. While no organization can predict every potential crisis, having a strong crisis management framework in place ensures that the business can survive, recover, and even thrive in the face of adversity. Crisis management is not just about survival—it's about demonstrating leadership, maintaining trust, and emerging stronger. By mastering the art of crisis management, businesses can ensure their long-term resilience and success.

FROGMAN MINDFULNESS

Jon Macaskill
US Navy SEAL Commander (Ret)
Keynote Speaking
One on One Coaching
Mindfulness Teaching
www.frogmanmindfulness.com
757-619-1211

Building a Resilient Leadership Framework for the Future

In an era marked by rapid change, technological advancements, and global challenges, resilient leadership has become a critical component for organizational success. Resilience is not just about bouncing back from setbacks, but also about being able to adapt, innovate, and lead through uncertainty. As businesses face an increasingly complex landscape, the need for leaders who can navigate disruption and lead with confidence has never been more essential.

Resilient leadership involves the ability to withstand and recover from adversity while maintaining focus on long-term goals. It requires a mindset that embraces change, empowers teams, and fosters a culture of continuous learning. Building a resilient leadership framework is about developing the capacity to not only survive but thrive, even in the face of the unexpected.

This article explores the characteristics of resilient leaders, the strategies they use to navigate crises, and how organizations can create a leadership framework that supports adaptability, innovation, and long-term success. By focusing on practical tips and real-world examples, we will show how organizations can foster resilient leadership at all levels to build a sustainable and thriving future.

What is Resilient Leadership?

Resilient leadership is defined as the ability of leaders to effectively respond to challenges, recover from setbacks, and maintain a clear sense of direction in the face of adversity. Resilient leaders possess several key traits that enable them to lead their teams through uncertainty and maintain focus on long-term goals despite immediate pressures. These leaders are able to adapt to changing circumstances, motivate their teams, and provide guidance during difficult times.

At its core, resilient leadership is about embracing change, demonstrating emotional intelligence, and fostering a culture of collaboration and continuous improvement. Leaders with resilience do not shy away from challenges but instead use these experiences as opportunities for growth and development—both for themselves and their teams.

Core Traits of Resilient Leaders

1. Adaptability: Resilient leaders are flexible and open to change. They understand that in today's world, change is inevitable, and they are willing to adjust their approach, processes, and strategies to meet evolving challenges.

2. Emotional Intelligence (EQ): Emotional intelligence is the ability to recognize and manage one's emotions and the emotions of others. Resilient leaders are empathetic, self-aware, and able to maintain composure under pressure. They inspire confidence and trust in their teams by remaining calm and collected, even during times of uncertainty.

3. Optimism and Positivity: Resilient leaders maintain a positive outlook, even in the face of adversity. They are solution-focused and emphasize the potential for growth and improvement, rather than dwelling on

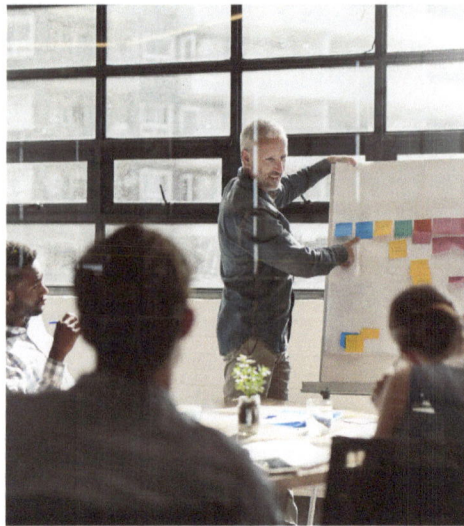

4. Decisiveness: During a crisis, leaders must be able to make quick, informed decisions. Resilient leaders are able to evaluate the available information, weigh the risks, and take decisive action. They understand that inaction can be just as harmful as making the wrong decision.

4. Visionary Thinking: Resilient leaders maintain a clear vision of the future and guide their teams towards long-term goals. They can articulate a compelling vision, even during times of uncertainty, and motivate others to align with that vision.

5. Self-Care and Balance: Resilient leaders understand the importance of self-care and work-life balance. They recognize that in order to lead effectively, they must first take care of themselves, both physically and emotionally. This ensures they have the stamina and energy to lead their teams through difficult

Why Resilient Leadership is Crucial for the Future

In today's business world, organizations face a multitude of challenges, from economic fluctuations and technological disruption to changing customer expectations and global crises. The need for resilient leadership is more urgent than ever, as companies must adapt quickly to survive and thrive in this volatile environment.

1. Navigating Uncertainty and Change. The pace of change in the business world is accelerating. Technological advancements, shifting market demands, and global disruptions have created an environment where organizations must continuously evolve to stay competitive. Resilient leadership enables organizations to navigate these changes effectively. Leaders who embrace change and demonstrate adaptability can help their teams remain flexible and innovative in response to market shifts.

Example: The COVID-19 pandemic demonstrated the importance of resilient leadership as companies were forced to adapt to remote work, supply chain disruptions, and changing customer needs. Leaders who quickly embraced digital transformation, supported their teams through uncertainty, and communicated effectively were better positioned to sustain their businesses and emerge stronger.

2. Enhancing Employee Engagement and Retention:

Resilient leaders are crucial for maintaining employee morale and engagement, especially during tough times. When employees see that their leaders can remain calm, decisive, and optimistic, they are more likely to stay motivated and committed to the organization. Resilient leadership fosters a culture of trust and psychological safety, where employees feel supported and empowered to perform at their best.

Case Study: During the financial crisis of 2008, many companies saw mass layoffs and workforce reductions. However, companies like Southwest Airlines and Zappos managed to retain employee loyalty by demonstrating transparency, clear communication, and a commitment to employee well-being. These companies maintained strong cultures of trust and support, which allowed them to weather the crisis and recover more quickly than their competitors.

3. Driving Innovation and Adaptation: Resilient leaders encourage creativity and

innovation, particularly during times of disruption. They are not afraid to take calculated risks or explore new ideas, and they foster a culture where experimentation is encouraged. This focus on innovation allows organizations to adapt to changing circumstances and capitalize on new opportunities.

Example: Apple's CEO, Tim Cook, led the company through a period of significant transformation following the death of founder Steve Jobs. Cook's resilient leadership allowed Apple to continue innovating with new products such as the Apple Watch, while also embracing new technologies like artificial intelligence and augmented reality. This innovation has been a key factor in Apple's continued growth and dominance in the tech industry.

Strategies for Building a Resilient Leadership Framework

Building a resilient leadership framework requires a strategic approach that focuses on developing the necessary skills, creating supportive structures, and fostering an organizational culture that promotes resilience at all levels. Below are key strategies that can help organizations build a resilient leadership framework:

1. Develop Leadership Training Programs Focused on Resilience: One of the most effective ways to build a resilient leadership framework is through training and development programs that focus on the key traits of resilient leaders. These programs should address topics such as emotional intelligence, decision-making under pressure, effective communication, and adaptability.

Actionable Step: Offer leadership development workshops and training that include scenario-based exercises, where leaders can practice making decisions in high-pressure situations. This helps develop their ability to think critically and lead with confidence during a crisis.

2. Foster a Culture of Psychological Safety: A culture of psychological safety is one in which employees feel comfortable taking risks, sharing ideas, and making mistakes without fear of retribution. Resilient leaders foster this environment by encouraging open communication, actively listening to employees, and creating a safe space for feedback.

Actionable Step: Encourage leaders to practice active listening and provide constructive feedback. Leaders should regularly check in with their teams to understand their concerns and provide support. This helps employees feel valued and enables them to contribute more effectively to problem-solving during times of uncertainty.

3. Focus on Building Strong Relationships and Trust:

Strong relationships are the foundation of resilient leadership. Leaders must build trust with their teams, stakeholders, and customers. This requires consistent communication, honesty, and a commitment to integrity. When employees trust their leaders, they are more likely to remain engaged and perform at their best, even during crises.

Actionable Step: Encourage leaders to build personal connections with their teams by taking the time to understand their needs and concerns. Leaders should be transparent about the organization's goals, challenges, and strategies for moving forward.

4. Embrace Flexibility and Agile Leadership:
Resilient leaders embrace flexibility and adaptability, especially during times of disruption. Agile leadership is about being able to pivot quickly, make informed decisions, and adjust strategies as necessary. Resilient leaders empower their teams to adapt to changing circumstances and find new ways to approach challenges.

Actionable Step: Implement agile leadership practices by allowing teams to work in cross-functional units, test ideas quickly, and adjust strategies based on feedback. Encourage leaders to support innovation and experimentation, even if it means stepping outside their comfort zones.

5. Prioritize Well-Being and Work-Life Balance:
Resilient leaders understand the importance of self-care and encourage their teams to prioritize their well-being. A focus on mental health, work-life balance, and stress management is critical for maintaining long-term resilience. Leaders who take care of themselves are better equipped to handle stress and guide their teams through tough times.

Actionable Step: Implement wellness programs that support employees' physical and mental health. Encourage leaders to model healthy behaviors, such as taking regular breaks, setting boundaries, and maintaining a work-life balance.

Real-World Examples of Resilient Leadership

1. Indra Nooyi at PepsiCo: Indra Nooyi, former CEO of PepsiCo, demonstrated remarkable resilience during her tenure at the company. Under her leadership, PepsiCo successfully navigated changing consumer preferences, economic downturns, and challenges in the global marketplace.

Nooyi's ability to balance short-term profitability with long-term sustainability initiatives helped PepsiCo remain a dominant player in the beverage industry. Her resilience was evident in her focus on innovation, strategic acquisitions, and expanding PepsiCo's product portfolio to include healthier options. She also championed diversity and inclusion at PepsiCo, ensuring that the company's workforce was representative of the global markets it served.

2. New Zealand's Prime Minister, Jacinda Ardern:

Jacinda Ardern has earned global recognition for her resilient leadership, particularly during the Christchurch mosque shootings and the COVID-19 pandemic. Her compassionate yet decisive response to the Christchurch tragedy—implementing swift gun control measures and providing comfort to the victims—highlighted her ability to lead with empathy and strength.

Ardern's leadership style demonstrates that resilience is not only about decisiveness in the face of crisis but also about fostering unity, demonstrating vulnerability, and providing hope in times of adversity.

Conclusion:

Building a resilient leadership framework is not a one-time effort—it's an ongoing process that requires continuous learning, adaptability, and a commitment to the well-being of both leaders and teams. Resilient leadership is critical for navigating the challenges of the future, ensuring that organizations remain flexible, innovative, and prepared for whatever comes next. In today's fast-paced business environment, where disruption is constant and the pace of change is accelerating, leaders who can adapt and thrive under pressure will be the ones who lead successful organizations into the future.

As the business landscape continues to evolve, resilient leaders will be the ones who guide their organizations through uncertainty, inspire their teams to reach new heights, and drive long-term success. By fostering a culture of trust, openness, and collaboration, they empower their teams to take initiative and find creative solutions to complex problems. Moreover, resilient leaders are not just focused on short-term achievements; they prioritize long-term goals and work diligently to ensure their teams are aligned with the organization's mission and values.

By developing the traits, strategies, and frameworks outlined in this article, organizations can build resilient leadership that fosters agility, innovation, and growth, enabling them to thrive in the face of adversity. A resilient leader creates an environment where employees feel supported, valued, and confident in their ability to navigate challenges, both individually and collectively.

Organizations that invest in building resilient leadership not only weather storms with greater ease but also emerge stronger, more unified, and better equipped to capitalize on new opportunities. Through ongoing reflection, learning, and a commitment to personal and organizational growth, resilient leadership becomes a key driver for sustainable success.

YOUR IDEAS ARE VALUABLE PROTECT THEM TODAY

Intellectual Property is the Most Valuable Part of your Business

Instant IP™

Limited Time Offer for Enterprise Level
Promo Code: jetlaunch

IP PROTECTION	TIME	MONEY
Patent	1-3 Years	$30,000
Instant IP	1 Minute	$97

FREE TRIAL – INSTANTIP.APP

The Evolution of Customer Experience: Trends and Innovations

In today's hyper-competitive business landscape, delivering an exceptional customer experience (CX) has become one of the most important differentiators for companies across industries. Customers have more options than ever before, and their expectations continue to rise. Gone are the days when businesses could get by with simply offering a good product or service; now, customers demand seamless, personalized, and efficient interactions at every touchpoint. The evolution of customer experience has moved from transactional service to emotional engagement, with businesses striving to build long-lasting relationships with their customers.

This article explores the evolution of customer experience, examining the trends, technologies, and innovations that have shaped CX over the years. We'll discuss how customer expectations have changed, the role of digital transformation in improving CX, and the strategies companies can implement to stay ahead of the curve. By understanding these trends and innovations, businesses can better meet the demands of today's savvy consumers and create memorable, impactful experiences that drive customer loyalty.

The Changing Landscape of Customer Expectations

Customer expectations have undergone a dramatic shift in recent years, driven by technological advancements, changing consumer behaviors, and increased access to information. The modern customer is informed, empowered, and more connected than ever before. With the advent of smartphones, social media, and e-commerce, customers now expect brands to be available 24/7, respond to inquiries in real-time, and provide personalized experiences.

1. The Rise of the Digital-First Customer: One of the most significant shifts in customer behavior has been the move to digital-first interactions. Today, customers expect to engage with businesses through digital channels such as websites, mobile apps, social media, and chatbots. The COVID-19 pandemic further accelerated this trend, with a significant increase in online shopping, virtual customer service interactions, and the adoption of digital payment methods.

The digital-first mindset has also led to the rise of omnichannel experiences, where customers expect a seamless transition between online and offline interactions. Whether customers are browsing a website, interacting with a chatbot, or making a purchase in-store, they expect the experience to be consistent, efficient, and convenient.

Example: Companies like Amazon and Apple have mastered the digital-first approach by providing customers with intuitive, user-friendly platforms that offer a seamless shopping experience. Amazon's recommendation engine, for example, uses customer data to personalize product suggestions, creating a more relevant and engaging shopping experience.

2. The Demand for Personalization: Another major shift in customer expectations is the increasing

demand for personalized experiences. With the vast amounts of data available to businesses today, customers expect companies to understand their needs, preferences, and behaviors in order to deliver tailored offerings. From personalized product recommendations to customized email marketing campaigns, customers expect businesses to speak to them as individuals.

Personalization is no longer a luxury; it has become an expectation. Customers want brands to anticipate their needs and provide relevant, targeted content and offers that are aligned with their specific interests. In fact, studies show that customers are more likely to make a purchase when they receive personalized recommendations or offers based on their past behaviors.

Case Study: Netflix is a prime example of personalization

done right. The streaming giant uses advanced algorithms to recommend shows and movies based on users' viewing history, preferences, and ratings. This level of personalization keeps customers engaged and encourages them to continue using the platform.

3. Real-Time Responses and Instant Gratification: Today's customers demand instant gratification. Whether they are looking for customer support, making a purchase, or engaging with a brand on social media, they expect fast responses and quick resolutions. The rise of instant messaging platforms and chatbots has set a new standard for real-time customer service, where waiting for a response is no longer acceptable.

Businesses that can provide fast, efficient service—whether it's through live chat, social media, or self-service options—are more likely to build trust and loyalty with their customers. Additionally, with the rise of mobile-first interactions, customers expect to have their needs met instantly and on-the-go.

Example: Zappos, an online retailer, is known for its exceptional customer service. The company's customer support team is available 24/7 via phone, email, and live chat, ensuring that customers can reach out at any time and receive prompt assistance. Zappos' commitment to real-time support has helped the company maintain high customer satisfaction levels.

Technological Innovations Shaping the Future of Customer Experience

Technology has played a pivotal role in the evolution of customer experience. From AI-powered chatbots to advanced data analytics, businesses are increasingly leveraging technology to enhance CX and meet customer expectations. Below are some of the key technological innovations that are transforming the customer experience landscape.

1. Artificial Intelligence and Machine Learning:

Artificial intelligence (AI) and machine learning (ML) are revolutionizing customer experience by enabling businesses to deliver more personalized, efficient, and proactive service. AI-driven

Additionally, AI and ML are used to analyze vast amounts of customer data, allowing businesses to predict customer behavior, identify trends, and offer tailored recommendations. By leveraging AI and ML, companies can improve decision-making, automate processes, and enhance the overall customer experience.

Case Study: Spotify uses AI and machine learning to provide personalized music recommendations to users. By analyzing listening history, user preferences, and collaborative playlists, Spotify is able to create curated playlists and offer music suggestions that resonate with individual users, enhancing their overall experience.

2. Chatbots and Virtual Assistants:

Chatbots and virtual assistants are becoming increasingly common tools for enhancing customer experience. These AI-driven tools can provide customers with instant responses to their inquiries, help them navigate websites, and resolve issues without human intervention. Chatbots are often used in customer service, sales, and marketing, providing customers with immediate assistance and freeing up human agents to focus on more complex tasks.

Virtual assistants, such as Amazon's Alexa or Apple's Siri, are also playing a significant role in transforming CX by providing voice-activated interactions that make it easier for customers to access information and perform tasks.

Example: H&M uses a chatbot called "Ada" to assist customers with inquiries about products, store locations, and order tracking. Ada can also recommend clothing items based on customers' preferences, making the shopping experience more personalized and convenient.

3. Omnichannel and Cross-Channel Experiences:

As customers interact with brands through multiple touchpoints—whether it's online, in-store, via social media, or over the phone—there is an increasing demand for a seamless, omnichannel experience. Customers expect to transition smoothly between different channels without having to repeat information or deal with inconsistencies in service.

An omnichannel approach integrates various communication channels to create a unified, consistent experience for customers. This approach allows businesses to provide personalized, relevant interactions no matter how or where customers engage.

Example: Starbucks has mastered the omnichannel approach by integrating its mobile app, in-store experience, and online ordering system. Customers can order coffee through the app, pay via their phones, and pick up their drinks in-store without any friction. This seamless experience has contributed to Starbucks' success in building customer loyalty.

4. Augmented Reality (AR) and Virtual Reality (VR):

Augmented reality (AR) and virtual reality (VR) are emerging technologies that are enhancing the customer experience in innovative ways. AR allows customers to interact with digital content overlaid onto the real world, while VR immerses users in fully digital environments. Both technologies are being used by businesses to engage customers in more interactive and memorable ways.

For example, AR is being used in retail to allow customers to virtually try on products, such as clothing, makeup, or furniture, before making a purchase. VR is being used in industries such as travel and real estate to offer virtual tours of destinations or properties.

Example: IKEA's AR app, "IKEA Place," allows customers to visualize how furniture would look in their homes by superimposing 3D models of products onto their living spaces through their smartphones. This innovative use of AR enhances the shopping experience and helps customers make more informed purchasing decisions.

Building a Customer-Centric Culture

While technology plays a significant role in enhancing customer experience, it is the organizational culture that drives the true success of CX initiatives. Building a customer-centric culture means putting the customer at the heart of everything the business does—from product development to marketing, sales, and customer support.

1. Empowering Employees to Deliver Exceptional Service:

A customer-centric culture is built on the foundation of empowered employees. When employees feel valued, supported, and equipped with the tools they need to succeed, they are more likely to deliver exceptional service to customers. Training programs, performance recognition, and a focus on employee well-being all contribute to creating an environment where employees are motivated to go above and beyond for customers.

Actionable Step: Provide employees with continuous training on customer service best practices and product knowledge. Encourage employees to take ownership of customer issues and resolve problems proactively.

2. Listening to Customer Feedback and Acting on It :

Customer feedback is a powerful tool for improving customer experience. Resilient organizations continuously gather feedback through surveys, reviews, social media interactions, and direct customer interactions. By actively listening to customers and addressing their concerns, businesses can refine their products, services, and customer support strategies.

Actionable Step: Implement a robust feedback loop that includes regular surveys, customer satisfaction measurements, and social media monitoring. Use this feedback to identify areas for improvement and adjust strategies accordingly.

3. Creating Emotional Connections with Customers:

Emotional connections are at the core of a positive customer experience. Customers are more likely to remain loyal to brands that make them feel valued and appreciated. By creating emotional connections through personalized interactions, companies can foster stronger relationships with their customers, leading to higher retention rates and increased customer lifetime value.

Example: Nike has built an emotional connection with its customers through its "Just Do It" campaign and focus on inspiring athletes of all levels. The brand encourages customers to push beyond their limits, creating a sense of community and shared values.

Conclusion:

The evolution of customer experience is a journey, not a destination. As technology continues to advance and customer expectations evolve, businesses must remain agile and responsive to these changes. The future of customer experience lies in creating personalized, seamless, and emotionally engaging interactions that resonate with customers at every touchpoint. Companies that succeed will be those that not only meet the immediate demands of today's customers but also anticipate future needs and stay ahead of the curve.

By embracing emerging technologies such as artificial intelligence, chatbots, and augmented reality, businesses can enhance the overall customer experience and offer more tailored, relevant services. However, technology alone is not enough. Fostering a customer-centric culture within the organization is essential for delivering experiences that truly resonate. Listening to customer feedback and adapting quickly to their needs will allow companies to stay competitive and create lasting emotional connections with their audience.

The businesses that lead in customer experience innovation will be those that integrate technology with empathy, listening, and consistent engagement. These organizations will set the stage for long-term success, customer loyalty, and sustained growth. As customer expectations continue to rise, the ability to adapt and deliver exceptional, personalized experiences will be the key to staying relevant and competitive in an ever-evolving marketplace.

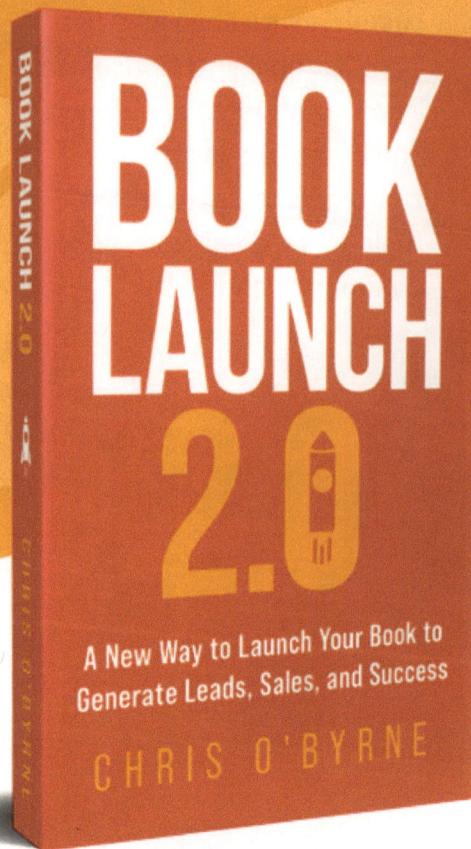

The Rise of Social Commerce: Integrating Shopping into Social Media

Over the last decade, social media has evolved from a tool for personal connection and communication into a powerful platform for business and commerce. With billions of active users across platforms such as Facebook, Instagram, TikTok, and Pinterest, social media is no longer just a space for social interactions—it has become a significant avenue for businesses to connect with consumers, showcase their products, and drive sales. The fusion of social media with e-commerce has given rise to social commerce, a rapidly growing trend that is transforming the retail landscape and reshaping the way consumers shop.

Social commerce refers to the process of using social media platforms to facilitate online purchasing and to create a seamless shopping experience. From shoppable Instagram posts to TikTok influencers promoting products, social commerce is revolutionizing the customer journey by integrating shopping directly into the platforms people already use every day. With its ability to combine entertainment, social interaction, and shopping into one cohesive experience, social commerce has gained traction as a key strategy for businesses looking to reach a more engaged, younger, and tech-savvy audience.

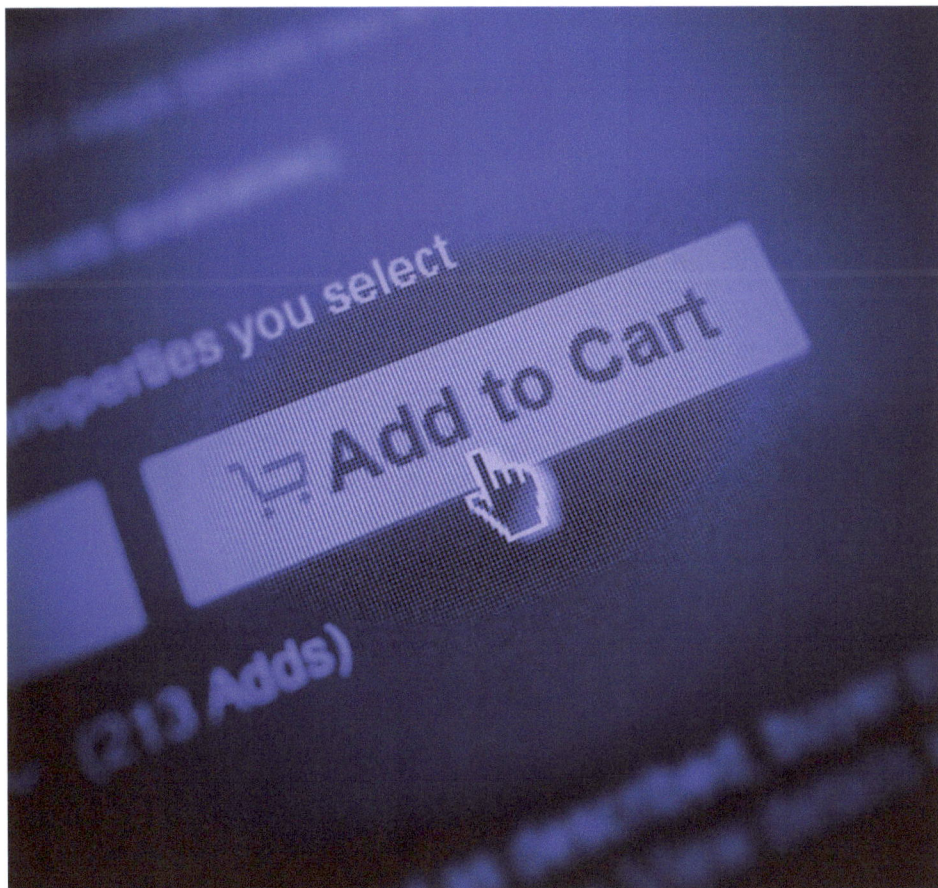

In this article, we will explore the rise of social commerce, its impact on consumer behavior and the retail industry, the key trends driving this shift, and the challenges businesses face as they navigate this new frontier of commerce. We will also look at the legal and ethical considerations that businesses must keep in mind as they adopt social commerce strategies, from data privacy to advertising regulations.

The Evolution of Social Commerce

Social media platforms have long been used as marketing tools, offering businesses an opportunity to reach large audiences through organic content and paid ads. However, traditional social media advertising was often disconnected from the purchasing process, requiring consumers to leave the platform and visit an external website to complete a purchase. This created friction in the customer journey, and businesses had to find new ways to convert social media engagement into actual sales.

The shift towards social commerce can be traced back to the early days of platforms like Instagram, where influencers and brands began using "shoppable posts" to drive sales directly from their feed. These posts allowed businesses to tag products in their images, creating a direct link to a product page where customers could purchase items without ever leaving the platform. This seamless shopping experience resonated with users, and social media platforms began building more integrated e-commerce features, such as Facebook Shops, Instagram's Shopping tab, and TikTok's "Shop Now" feature.

As social media platforms began incorporating more shopping capabilities, the rise of influencer marketing and user-generated content further fueled the growth of social commerce. Influencers, who were already promoting products on social media, began driving significant traffic to online stores by featuring products in their posts, videos, and stories. Brands realized the power of these authentic, peer-to-peer

recommendations and began partnering with influencers to create sponsored content that would resonate with their followers.

Key Milestones in the Rise of Social Commerce

- 2015: Instagram introduced shoppable posts, allowing brands to tag products directly in images and posts.
- 2017: Facebook launched Facebook Marketplace, enabling users to buy and sell items directly within the platform.
- 2019: Instagram introduced Instagram Checkout, allowing users to complete purchases without leaving the app.
- 2020: TikTok launched its own e-commerce features, including shoppable ads and live-stream shopping events, in collaboration with brands like Walmart.
- 2021: Facebook Shops was rolled out, enabling businesses to create online storefronts on both Facebook and Instagram, streamlining the social commerce experience.

These milestones reflect a broader trend of social media platforms

evolving from communication and entertainment hubs to integrated, multi-functional commerce platforms.

The Impact of Social Commerce on Consumer Behavior

Social commerce is transforming the way consumers discover, engage with, and purchase products. As social media platforms increasingly become shopping destinations, businesses are learning how to tap into the power of these platforms to drive sales and build brand loyalty.

1. The Social Media Shopping Experience: One of the most significant advantages of social commerce is its ability to combine discovery and purchase in a single, frictionless experience. Consumers no longer have to search for products across multiple platforms or wait for a promotional email to find deals. With social commerce, product discovery happens organically through the content consumers are already engaging with—whether it's an influencer's post, a brand's video, or an interactive poll on Instagram Stories.

This seamless integration of shopping into social media allows users to make impulse purchases based on emotional engagement with the content. For example, a user may see a post about a new skincare product on Instagram, watch a quick demonstration, and then click the "Shop Now" button to buy it. The ability to buy directly from the post eliminates the need to leave the platform and reduces friction in the customer journey.

2. Social Proof and Peer Recommendations:
The power of social proof in driving consumer behavior cannot be underestimated. Social media platforms thrive on user-generated content, where consumers share their experiences, reviews, and opinions on products. When a customer sees their friends, family, or influencers endorsing a product, it creates a sense of trust and credibility, which can strongly influence purchasing decisions.

Influencers and user-generated content have become crucial components of social commerce.

Influencers are seen as authentic, relatable figures who provide honest reviews and recommendations. As consumers increasingly turn to social media for product recommendations, businesses are embracing the opportunity to partner with influencers to promote their products in an authentic and engaging way.

3. The Rise of Video Shopping and Live Streaming:
Another trend that is reshaping consumer behavior is the use of video content to drive sales. Social media platforms like Instagram, TikTok, and Facebook are increasingly incorporating live-streaming features that allow brands to showcase products in real-time and engage with customers directly. This format provides an immersive and interactive experience, where consumers can ask questions, view product demonstrations, and purchase products during the live stream.

Live shopping events have become particularly popular on platforms like TikTok, where influencers and brands host interactive sessions where viewers can make instant purchases as they watch.

This trend is especially popular among younger audiences, who enjoy the entertainment value and the ability to interact with brands in real time.

Key Trends Driving Social Commerce
Several key trends are contributing to the rapid growth of social commerce and shaping the future of online shopping. These trends include the integration of technology, the rise of influencer marketing, and the growing importance of data-driven personalization.

1. Influencer Marketing and Collaborative Content:
Influencer marketing has played a significant role in the rise of social commerce. With their loyal followers and authentic voices, influencers have become powerful conduits for promoting products and driving sales. Social media platforms have responded to this trend by providing brands with tools to collaborate with influencers on sponsored content and affiliate marketing.

Influencers can now seamlessly tag products in their posts, creating direct shopping links and facilitating conversions. These collaborations often lead to higher levels of engagement and more effective calls to action.

2. Integration of Augmented Reality (AR):
Augmented reality (AR) is one of the most exciting technologies driving social commerce forward. AR allows consumers to virtually try on products, such as makeup or clothing, before making a purchase. For example, Instagram's AR filters allow users to "try on" lipstick shades or see how a piece of furniture would

look in their homes.

By incorporating AR technology into social media platforms, brands can create immersive shopping experiences that enhance customer engagement and make it easier for consumers to make purchase decisions.

3. Artificial Intelligence and Data-Driven Personalization:

Artificial intelligence (AI) is transforming the way businesses personalize the shopping experience on social media platforms. By analyzing consumer data, AI algorithms can suggest products based on users' past behavior, preferences, and engagement with the brand's content. This hyper-targeted approach to advertising and product recommendations increases the likelihood of conversions and enhances the overall customer experience. Social media platforms like Facebook and Instagram are increasingly leveraging AI to offer personalized ad experiences, ensuring that the right products reach the right people at the right time.

Challenges and Considerations for Businesses in Social Commerce

While the rise of social commerce offers significant opportunities for businesses, it also comes with its own set of challenges.

Companies must navigate issues such as data privacy concerns, regulatory compliance, and the potential for over saturation in a highly competitive space.

1. Data Privacy and Security: As businesses collect more data through social media interactions, ensuring that customer data is handled securely becomes increasingly important. Social media platforms collect vast amounts of data on users, and businesses must be mindful of data privacy regulations such as the GDPR (General Data Protection Regulation) in Europe and CCPA (California Consumer Privacy Act) in the United States.

Failure to comply with data privacy regulations can result in heavy fines and damage to the company's reputation. Businesses must implement robust data protection measures and be transparent with customers about how their data will be used.

2. Platform Dependency and Algorithm Changes: A significant risk for businesses that rely heavily on social commerce is the potential for changes in platform algorithms. Social media platforms frequently update their algorithms, affecting the visibility of content and the effectiveness of paid ads. Businesses that rely on organic reach or paid promotions must be prepared for these changes, which can impact their ability to drive traffic and

sales.

3. Competition and Oversaturation: As more businesses enter the social commerce space, standing out in a crowded market becomes a challenge. Brands must find innovative ways to capture attention and engage their audiences. Whether through influencer partnerships, creative content, or offering exclusive promotions, businesses need to differentiate themselves to succeed in the competitive social commerce environment.

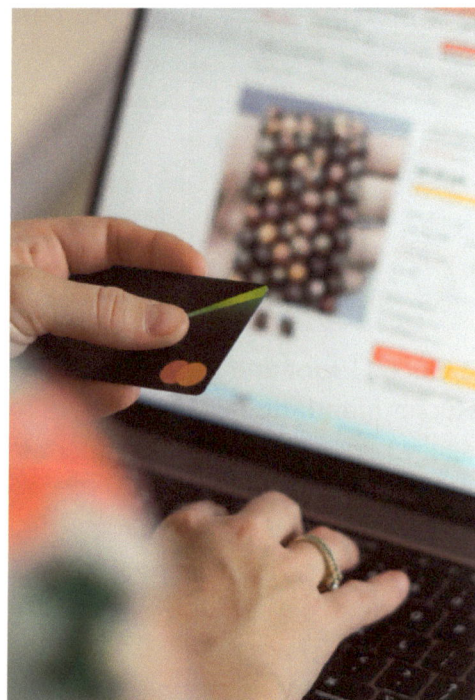

The Future of Social Commerce

The future of social commerce looks bright, with continued growth expected as social media platforms evolve and new technologies emerge. As businesses continue to innovate and leverage social platforms to engage with consumers, we can expect even more seamless integration of shopping experiences into social media.

1. Expanding E-Commerce Features Across Platforms:

As more platforms integrate e-commerce features, businesses will have greater opportunities to reach customers across multiple touch points. This expansion will further blur the lines between social media and shopping, offering consumers even more ways to interact with brands and make purchases.

2. The Role of Virtual Reality and AI in Shaping Social Commerce:

As technology continues to advance, the role of virtual reality (VR) and artificial intelligence (AI) in social commerce will continue to grow. VR will enable consumers to explore products in immersive virtual environments, while AI will continue to provide personalized shopping experiences based on real-time data.

Conclusion:

The rise of social commerce represents a significant shift in how consumers shop and interact with brands. Social media platforms have transformed from merely socializing spaces to powerful commerce hubs, where users can seamlessly discover, explore, and purchase products—all within the same platform. As platforms like Instagram, TikTok, and Facebook continue to integrate e-commerce features, businesses are presented with unparalleled opportunities to create more personalized, seamless, and engaging shopping experiences for their customers. This shift is enabling brands to connect with audiences in ways that were once only achievable through traditional brick-and-mortar retail experiences.

However, the growth of social commerce also brings new challenges. Businesses must remain agile in navigating complex issues such as data privacy, platform dependency, and the growing competition in this crowded marketplace. As the use of customer data becomes more integrated into social commerce strategies, maintaining privacy and adhering to regulations like GDPR and CCPA is crucial. Furthermore, relying too heavily on a single platform or influencer can create vulnerabilities if algorithms or platform rules change.

To succeed in social commerce, businesses must embrace emerging technologies like artificial intelligence, augmented reality, and live-streaming to enhance the shopping experience and stay relevant to their audience. Integrating these technologies into their strategies will not only improve customer engagement but also increase sales and brand loyalty.

As social commerce continues to evolve, businesses that innovate while maintaining a customer-first approach will lead the way in this dynamic, ever-changing landscape.

In conclusion, the future of commerce is undeniably social. By adapting to these trends, businesses can position themselves for sustained success and growth in the digital era of retail.